T0278188

FLEX

FLEX

FLEX

Smart Strategies to Build a Successful Career Around Your Life

ELIZABETH WILLETTS

WILEY

This edition first published 2025

© 2025 John Wiley & Sons Ltd.

All rights reserved, including rights for text and data mining and training of artificial technologies or similar technologies. No part of this publication may be reproduced, stored in a retrieval system, or transmitted, in any form or by any means, electronic, mechanical, photocopying, recording or otherwise, except as permitted by law. Advice on how to obtain permission to reuse material from this title is available at http://www.wiley.com/go/permissions.

The right of Elizabeth Willetts to be identified as the author of this work has been asserted in accordance with law.

Registered Office(s)
John Wiley & Sons, Inc., 111 River Street, Hoboken, NJ 07030, USA
John Wiley & Sons Ltd, New Era House, 8 Oldlands Way, Bognor Regis, West Sussex, PO22 8NQ, UK

For details of our global editorial offices, customer services, and more information about Wiley products visit us at www.wiley.com.

Wiley also publishes its books in a variety of electronic formats and by print-on-demand. Some content that appears in standard print versions of this book may not be available in other formats.

Trademarks: Wiley and the Wiley logo are trademarks or registered trademarks of John Wiley & Sons, Inc. and/or its affiliates in the United States and other countries and may not be used without written permission. All other trademarks are the property of their respective owners. John Wiley & Sons, Inc. is not associated with any product or vendor mentioned in this book.

Limit of Liability/Disclaimer of Warranty

While the publisher and authors have used their best efforts in preparing this work, they make no representations or warranties with respect to the accuracy or completeness of the contents of this work and specifically disclaim all warranties, including without limitation any implied warranties of merchantability or fitness for a particular purpose. No warranty may be created or extended by sales representatives, written sales materials or promotional statements for this work. This work is sold with the understanding that the publisher is not engaged in rendering professional services. The advice and strategies contained herein may not be suitable for your situation. You should consult with a specialist where appropriate. The fact that an organization, website, or product is referred to in this work as a citation and/or potential source of further information does not mean that the publisher and authors endorse the information or services the organization, website, or product may provide or recommendations it may make. Further, readers should be aware that websites listed in this work may have changed or disappeared between when this work was written and when it is read. Neither the publisher nor authors shall be liable for any loss of profit or any other commercial damages, including but not limited to special, incidental, consequential, or other damages.

Library of Congress Cataloging-in-Publication Data is Available:

ISBN 9781394267798 (Paperback)
ISBN 9781394267835 (ePub)
ISBN 9781394267842 (ePDF)

Cover Design: Wiley
Cover Image: © vika_k/Adobe Stock Photos

Set in 11/16pt and ITCGaramondStd by Straive, Chennai, India
SKY10092516_120224

For my daughters, Emily and Annabelle – everything is for you! I hope I've shown you that anything is possible. Keep reaching for the stars!

Contents

In the final stretch of my therapy sessions, the focus shifted to preparing me for my return to work.

Seventeen months had passed since I took maternity leave at the height of my career to welcome my son into the world. Six months after my initial attempt to return to my role – a job at which I excelled – I found myself reduced to a mere shadow of my former self due to my organization's refusal to embrace flexible working arrangements.

It took a monumental battle, union intervention, a grievance, countless tears, and the support of my husband before I felt strong enough to go back. But when I did, I kept my promises and delivered results beyond expectations. I demonstrated that motherhood hadn't diminished my capabilities; if anything, it had enhanced them. I proved that reduced hours didn't equate to reduced ability and that I could deliver exceptional results in my senior leadership role.

But if I'm honest, I had mentally checked out.

I decided I deserved more than to be underestimated, doubted, and made to feel inadequate for wanting both a career and to be a mum. So, I redirected my energy towards retraining as a coach and mentor for women, helping them advance their careers and secure the salaries, success, and recognition they deserved.

This is when I met the mighty Elizabeth Willetts.

I first noticed Liz on LinkedIn. I was instantly drawn to her warmth, friendliness, and fierce passion for elevating women in the workforce. I detected a familiar Yorkshire accent (albeit a slightly posher one than mine!) and knew I had to reach out. We connected immediately and, after months of supporting and championing each other's work on the platform, began collaborating on various projects. The rest, as they say, is history.

Liz is an absolute powerhouse.

She is unwavering in her commitment to investing in you as a woman and helping you succeed in your career. Her extensive qualifications and experience uniquely position her to help you secure a well-paid, rewarding job that offers the flexibility you need and deserve.

Liz tirelessly partners with forward-thinking, family-friendly organizations that recognize the value of flexible working. She's not just a champion for gender equality; she's a force for change, working directly with companies to help them recruit and retain exceptional female talent – like you.

But here's the most important reason you should read this book: Liz gets it.

She knows firsthand how challenging it can be to secure a part-time role without taking a step down or accepting a significant pay cut – because she's been there herself. Liz, being Liz, decided that something needed to change and took matters into her own hands.

Fast forward five years, and Liz *IS* the change.

She's founded Investing in Women, a recruitment company and jobs board specifically for women, bridging the gap between talented women and progressive companies. She's making a significant impact on the UK's gender pay gap and has helped thousands of women find flexible part-time work they love.

In addition, Liz has built a community of over 60,000 like-minded women, paving the way for a brighter professional future for women everywhere, one hire at a time.

I told you she was a powerhouse!

I can't wait for her daughters, Emily and Annabelle, to grow up and realise how much their mum has done for them and for working women everywhere.

And I can't wait for you to get stuck into this book!

Liz has crammed over 18 years of recruitment experience into this masterpiece, covering everything you need – from figuring out your next career move to making an impact when you land that dream job, and everything in between. She's also brought in professional insights from her vast network of industry experts to fast-track your progress and skyrocket your results.

This is the book I needed all those years ago when I went on maternity leave, and it's the one you need today.

So, dive in, dig deep, and discover everything you need to know to keep your career on track when life gets in the way.

I'm so excited for you.

Leanne Cooper
Founder, You First Coaching Ltd
July 2024

Acknowledgements

Wow – where to start? First of all, I would like to say a huge thank you to the publishing and editing team at Wiley for all their help and support. This is my first (but hopefully not my last) book, and the team has always been on hand to answer any questions I may have. Big thanks to Tom Dinse, Alice Hadaway, Stacey Rivera, and Gemma Valler, who believed in the book's vision before I'd even written a word!

Of course, I have to say a HUGE thank you to Up the Gains' Sammie Ellard-King, who very kindly invited me to guest speak on his podcast, The Money Gains. By chance, a member of the editing team at Wiley listened to it, leading to this book!

This book would not be here without the incredibly rich conversations I've had with countless guests on my Work It Like A Mum podcast and LinkedIn Lives. A big thank you to all those who allowed their stories and advice to be featured in this book, including Leanne Cooper, Roz Hobley, Lizzie Martin, Rosie Reynolds, Sarah McMath, Jen Smollett, Rachel Exton, Jodie Mason, Tiggy Atkinson, Charlotte Ralph, Donna Patterson, Nicola Lee, Ali Fanshawe, Christa Davies, Leigh Welsh, Rebecca Newenham, Tom Stenner-Evans, Laurie Macpherson, Laura Walker, Chloe Fletcher, Amanda Henderson, and Rose-Marie Fox. The book is all the more valuable and relatable because of your contributions.

To Adele McNicholl for literally keeping the Investing in Women show on the road, allowing me time to write this book. Thank you so much for all the candidate sourcing, interviewing, sharing jobs and account management. You are so much more than a colleague! Thank you!

Thank you so much to my lovely mum, Ann, who has provided us with countless hours of unpaid babysitting since launching my business and writing this book. She's always there if I need her – and does an amazing job looking after not just my children but also me! Thank you!

To my husband, Henry, who has supported Investing in Women from the very beginning. He gave me the confidence to give it a go, understood when I had to work late, and is always on hand for business advice. He is the best friend and father for our children I could wish for. I love doing life with you! Finally, this book is for my daughters, Emily and Annabelle. It was only when I became a mum that I realised how difficult it is to juggle work and family and how workplaces are not set up for those with caring responsibilities who may want to work flexibly. Ever since, I've been on a mission to educate employers about the benefits flexible working can bring. But I'm also determined to show my daughters that no matter what others say, our careers don't have to stop after children. In fact, it is often the start of a brand-new, magical chapter.

Introduction

'It doesn't look good.' I can feel the doctor moving the cold, hard probe around inside me. He's trying to get a better look.

I stare up at the plain, white ceiling.

My heart's beating so loudly that I'm surprised no one else has mentioned that they can hear the 'thud, thud, thud' pounding from my chest.

I pray to a God I don't believe in that I misheard the words. I wish with every fibre of my being for him to take those words back – words that have shattered what feels like my reason for living.

I continue to lay in silence, clutching my husband's hand so hard my knuckles turn white.

Finally, after what feels like an eternity, the doctor says the words I've been dreading to hear – 'I can't find a heartbeat.'

Say hello and welcome to your new career bestie as this book aims to have your back, no matter what life throws at you. In it, you'll find a mix of my own job searching and career advice – gained from 18 years in the recruitment business, tales from the recruitment front line, plus inspiring real-life case studies from people who have navigated life's unexpected twists and turns – and STILL managed to thrive in their careers. But this book isn't just about sharing stories (no matter how inspirational): it's about giving you the tools and confidence to navigate your own career path, whether you want to climb that ladder, need to take a step back, or pivot entirely. Inside, you'll find practical steps to dust off your CV, nail that interview, and balance a job you love with a busy life you love even more! Ready to get started? Let's dive in and build that dream career of yours, step by step. I'm with you every step of the way!

* * *

I'd never been overly career-ambitious, but I enjoyed working and the satisfaction that came with doing a good job. I was also good at my job and thrived in the fast-paced world of recruitment. I became one of the top performers in the City of London branch of one of the world's largest recruitment agencies. Here, I recruited accountants for some of the world's largest banks. I quickly rose through the ranks and, by the age of 24, was managing a team.

But the hours were long and the work demanding. Having been brought up by a traditional stay-at-home mum, I couldn't see how such a demanding job would work when I became a mum. And becoming a mum was ultimately what I wanted to be. When I got married a couple of years later, I checked out of my career before we even started trying for children! Silly right?!? I didn't realise it would take four and a half years of trying, a miscarriage and eventually IVF to realise my dream of parenthood. Hindsight's a wonderful thing, eh?

So I left my recruitment career without a backward glance (or so I thought) and set myself up as a beauty therapist and personal stylist through Colour Me Beautiful, working from home, a set-up I thought would work perfectly around my, at this point, make-believe family.

But after one and a half years of nada – not even the faintest line on a pregnancy test, and painful 'Are you planning to have children' questions from well-meaning clients, I went scurrying back to my old job with my tail firmly between my legs. It felt like I was back where I started, but in my absence, my juniors had been promoted ahead of me, and my best clients distributed to my colleagues. I really was starting again right at the bottom.

And my heart just wasn't in it anymore. I felt cheated being back – this wasn't the life I'd dreamed of. I no longer had the passion or felt the same connection to my clients or candidates. It was just a job that paid the bills. For a year and a half, I just trod water. Got up, went to work, came home, ate, watched tv, bed, repeat.

But then the miscarriage happened, my boss got pregnant, and watching her growing belly became increasingly painful. I knew now was the time to move on. Because children may or may not have happened for me, but work, work was there. It took up 90% of my waking hours, so I needed to enjoy it, right?

And, after what felt like countless interviews, I was finally offered my dream job as an in-house recruiter at one of the Big 4 accounting firms, and that's when things finally started to look up for me.

Joining such a corporate firm, which seemed to really value its staff, was a breath of fresh air. They even had an onsite gym and WFH (work from home), before anyone else knew what those three little letters stood for! And I spent a year or so healing – making friends, looking after my health, and getting good at my job. I met my stakeholders, earned their trust, and delivered excellent service. Once more, I took pride in my work, and although we were still 'trying for a baby', it didn't feel quite as desperate as it had when I thought a baby would be a 'get out of jail free card' from a job I hated.

Once I felt strong enough, we decided to try IVF and could not believe our luck when, on the second round, it worked. Nine months later, our daughter was born, and then – even more extraordinary – we got pregnant naturally a few months later.

So there I was, with two small kids, about to go back to work, when boom, a pandemic hit! Yep, I don't think any of us saw that coming! And, like many others, I found my job on the chopping block and was made redundant.

And that was that – my career was over – or so it felt. I'd listen to my husband on work calls with other adults. Work calls I wouldn't have thought twice about, but they suddenly sounded so glamorous and stimulating when I was up to my elbows in Play-Doh!

And with my eldest about to start pre-school, I knew I wanted to get back to work – working with other adults and feeling the thrill of recruitment again. But could I find another job that offered me the flexibility I wanted with two small children? Could I heck!

I'd chat with my friends who were dropping out of the workforce like flies, leaving well-paid careers having spent their 20s climbing the ladder to take something lower paid and lower skilled in exchange for the flexibility they wanted/desired.

I looked back on my recruitment career and realised that of the hundreds of people I'd placed, I'd never hired anyone into a part-time role. I'd been part of the problem! So I vowed to use my small redundancy payout of £5,000 to help people like me – and my friends. Those who enjoyed work, were diligent employees, and wanted to contribute to society and business but just needed something more flexible to fit around their lives – but didn't want to be punished with low-paid or low-skilled work because they also had other commitments.

So, I spent several months planning and writing business plans (that I've not looked at since) before founding Investing in Women – now a multi-award-winning job board and recruitment agency that helps forward-thinking organisations find talent looking for flexible and part-time work. Through our jobs board and free resources, we've helped thousands of people find flexible work that works around them and their lives.

In addition to offering our recruitment services, we host weekly Facebook and LinkedIn Lives with guest experts to help empower people to take control of their careers. Previous topics covered have included 'How to successfully return to work after maternity leave', 'Writing a CV recruiters will love', 'I hate my job – what should I do?', and 'Interview skills hiring managers are looking for right now', as well as several Lives with employment solicitors centred around discrimination at work and your rights to flexible working.

As well as our LinkedIn Lives, I host a weekly podcast called Work It Like A Mum, where I've interviewed some phenomenal women who have overcome various challenges, including cancer, raising four children under five!, baby loss, imposter syndrome, a lack of confidence and lengthy career breaks, but are now smashing it in the world of work. Some of their stories will be shared in this book.

I've also helped thousands of individuals land their dream jobs through my career coaching. Services include CV writing; LinkedIn profile building and strategy advice; interview confidence boosting sessions, as well as a career crossroads consultation for those feeling stuck in their career and don't know what they want to do. In these sessions, I help people identify their most valuable skills and experience and unravel what their dream career looks like — and a clear path on how to get it. A lot of the advice I give to my clients will be shared with you in this book so you too, can achieve the career you always dreamt of.

I've shared my story because I want you to know that sometimes, life gets in the way. Work and our careers aren't always our number one priority – and that's okay. It's normal, and it's life. And if you find that your focus is elsewhere, you're not alone. In fact, even some of the UK's leading CEOs haven't always been racing up that career ladder at 60 mph...

Sarah McMath[1] is a great example of viewing your career as a marathon, not a sprint. Whilst her children were small, she took several sideways steps in her career to roles that offered more flexibility. Here's what she had to say about that period of her career:

'I was clear I wanted to be a mum, and I also wanted to carry on working. No part of me considered stopping work. But I think that's hard in a working mum context. My children are now 20 and 18, but if I think about my mum friends, none returned to full-time work after having children. I didn't either at first, but nobody went back into the job they'd left for very long. Some of them did for a short period of time and then either changed careers or gave up work completely. So when I first went back, I worked three days a week. I did three days a week for about three years. And my husband went to four days a week. We found that worked well for us. But my experience when I went back was nobody on my team had really thought about it. I think I was a bit odd in that I was (one of the only women) in the team anyway, and then coming back after maternity leave was even harder.

I'd gone from being in a very senior position with a lot of responsibility and was suddenly asked to do more junior tasks. But I decided to take ownership of my career. And so entered this slightly weird phase of my career where I chased pregnant women. I would see another woman I didn't know very well at the coffee machine, very heavily pregnant, and ask her, "Well, who's covering your maternity leave?" She could be from a completely different department. I'd never worked with her before. Sometimes – I didn't know her name. And I'd say to my boss, "Well, they haven't sorted anything out, so I'm going off to cover their job next week."

But it was brilliant. I actually covered three different people's maternity leaves in three different parts of the business and learnt loads because they were things I would never have normally got involved with.'

While some of these roles weren't particularly stretching, they meant Sarah kept her foot in the door. Once her children started school and she had more time, she could put her foot back on the pedal and progress higher in her career. Sarah is now CEO of MOSL (the market operator for the non-household water retail market) in the male-dominated water industry.

Like Sarah, I've also learnt that our lives and careers are a marathon – not a sprint. Some years, you'll be going hell for leather, raising your hand for every promotion going – and others, you'll tread water or even feel like you're going backwards. It's during those times when you do decide you want to relight your career spark again that this book will be there to hold your hand. I'll use my 18+ years of recruitment experience to guide you through how to identify suitable jobs based on your skills, experience and interests, craft the perfect CV and a standout cover letter, and use LinkedIn to build a network and personal brand so that dream job literally lands in your inbox; how to have a standout interview so you become the unforgettable candidate, negotiate your job offer like a boss and return well to the workplace – no matter how long your career break. Please take notes as you go. I've crafted all the advice in this book to be actionable so you can create a career that you truly adore – one that stretches you (in the best possible way), lights you up and slots perfectly into your life.

Are you ready? Because here.we.go!

Note

1. Elizabeth Willetts (2022). How to Get What You Really Want in Your Career – Top Tips from a CEO Who's Made It to the Top of Her Male-Dominated Industry – Whilst Working Part-Time. *Work It Like A Mum* (podcast) 24 November 2022. MP3 audio, 48.07, www.buzzsprout .com/2046830/11663396. Accessed 1 August 2024.

Chapter 1

What Do You Want?

I'm assuming that many of you are reading this book because you feel stuck in your career and want to make a change. You might be on a career break, feel stuck in a role you just 'fell into', or work at a company with a toxic culture you want out of.

I get lots of messages from people who tell me that although they want to leave their current job, they don't know what to do. So, if this is you, I want you to know that you're not alone. Lots of us become adults and still don't know what we want to do when we 'grow up'.

In this chapter, I'm going to talk about how you can get clarity on what you want to do in your career – and how to reach it.

Evaluate Your Strengths

I firmly believe that we enjoy what we're good at. No one wants to feel out of their comfort zone all the time (although this is normal in the early days of any new job), or pretending to be someone they're not. Therefore, one of the first things I recommend you do is a personality strengths test so you learn what you're naturally good at and what will make you tick. You can take a personality test like this through a company called Gallup. Here's what Gallup says about the importance of personality strengths in their book *Now, Discover Your Strengths*:[1]

> *'Many people have little sense of their talents and strengths, much less the ability to build their lives around them. Instead,*

they are raised and taught to become experts in their weaknesses – and spend their lives trying to fix them while their strengths lie dormant.

Led by Don Clifton, the Father of Strengths-Based Psychology, Gallup created a revolutionary program to help people identify their talents; develop them into strengths; and enjoy consistent, near-perfect performance.'

At the heart of the Gallup programme is a CliftonStrengths assessment, which is available on their website, gallup.com. Their book *Now, Discover Your Strengths*, which accompanies the assessment, is a brilliant read that will enable you to get further clarity on the different strengths and personalities that make up the human psyche – great if you manage or work in a team.

According to Gallup, the CliftonStrengths assessment is 'the product of decades of research and hundreds of thousands of interviews to identify the most prevalent human strengths. There are 34 dominant talent themes . . . or patterns of human talent . . . and used with insight and understanding, [they] help capture the unique themes playing in each person's life'.

Once you've done your personality assessment and identified your strengths, use them. According to Gallup, 'The real tragedy in life is not that each of us doesn't have enough strengths. It's that we fail to use the ones we have.'

I took their strengths-based test, and it was eye-opening – one of the best things I've ever done. Suddenly, my whole personality made sense, and since then, I've made a conscious effort to lean into my strengths and worry less about any 'weaknesses' – delegating tasks that I know I'm no good at, don't serve my personality, and that I don't enjoy to others. I also no longer feel the need to apologise for who I am.

Gallup says that our personality traits will be in place by the age of three! Roz Hobley,[2] a leadership and performance coach with GiANT London, agrees:

'The wonderful thing about our personalities and wiring is that it doesn't change. So whether you're reading this as a university student, a mum at home who is going back or just gone back to work, your tendencies, the things that you naturally excel at, will always be there. Being a person of influence, where you can leave a real impact and legacy starts with understanding yourself – what you're like and can bring at your best, and also how you can undermine yourself.'

Rather than fighting those traits and working on our 'weaknesses' to become more rounded people, we should lean into our strengths. Do you think top CEOs like Elon Musk, Mark Zuckerberg, and Richard Branson worry about their 'personality weaknesses'? No, they have a strong sense of who they are and play to their strengths.

On the Diary of a CEO podcast, Branson, who suffers from dyslexia and left school at 15, explained this point to host Steven Bartlett, who recounted the tale in his book *Diary of a CEO*:[3]

'I was dyslexic and pretty hopeless at school; I just assumed that I must be a little bit thick. I could just about add up and subtract. But when it got to more complicated stuff I couldn't.

I was in a board meeting at about 50 years old, and I said to the director, is that good news or bad news? And one of the directors said, "Come outside, Richard". I came outside, and he said, "You don't know the difference between net profit and gross profit, do you?"

I said, "No".

He said, "I thought not", and brought out a sheet of paper and some colouring pens, and he colours it in blue, and then he puts a fishing net in it, and then he puts a little fish in the fishing net. And he says, "So, the fish that are in the net, that's your profit at the end of the year, and the rest of the ocean, that's your gross turnover". And I went, "I got it".'

What Do You Want?

But as Richard explains, it doesn't matter – it doesn't matter that he doesn't understand the difference between gross and net profit. He has leaned into his strength of being a visionary and bringing exciting products to market. And although he knows how to add up and subtract, he has left the accounting of his business to his Finance Director, who has, in turn, leaned into their strength.

Now, I'm not suggesting you want to be a FTSE 100 CEO or the next tech billionaire, but I firmly believe that those who lean into their strengths through their career choices are far more likely to thrive at work and be happier and healthier individuals.

Once you know your personality strengths, you can start making active choices about the types of roles that may suit you – or start making plans to get there if you're doing something completely different.

Roz[4] agrees and has the following advice:

'Something that we all strive for and can be very doable is to look at what are the things that you love and that you're good at and how you can incorporate them into your life personally and professionally. And we've used a tool at GiANT – it's actually really simple, called the 70/30, which says if you can spend 70% of your time doing activities or with people that give you life, that you're good at, that are energising or rewarding, you will always have the energy to spend 30% of your time, taking out the trash, doing the accounts, whatever activities that drain you.'

So, if you know you get your energy from being with lots of different people, you can look for roles that tick those boxes – receptionist, event manager, PR, recruitment, or sales, for example.

Or perhaps, through your personality assessment, you've discovered that you are a risk-averse introvert. Therefore, you know you would perform better in a home-based role or quiet office with a risk-averse element that complements your personality, like a legal, risk, compliance, or insurance specialist.

Maybe you're a do-er and would get frustrated in a public sector environment with lots of bureaucracy, or perhaps your caring traits have shone through in your results, and you know a role caring or helping others would be perfect for you.

Here's your action plan for today:

- Do your personality strengths-based assessment.
- Spend time digesting the results.

Right, off you go and prepare to be amazed!

Once you've done your test, write your results and any notes about your personality type in the box below:

```




```

Putting Your Strengths to Work

Welcome back to the book. I hope you found the personality test as valuable as I did.

Now it's time to analyse your personality strengths and what it means for you and your career. Think about which jobs might suit each personality strength – keep this quite objective initially – pretend you're doing it for a friend and just brainstorm. Use the box below to add at least 10–15 jobs for each of your strengths:

Now it's time to consider which jobs out of the ones you've thought of would light you up the most – and would complement your existing skill set and career history. Look at your current CV (don't worry, later in the book I will go through the entire step-by-step to create an interview-winning CV, plus there's a free CV template you can use at the back of the book) and identify, based on your previous experience, which positions that appeal to you the most you have the most transferable skills for (i.e. the most chance of getting).

So, you've got a list of potential jobs – it's now time to think about potential and dream industries/companies. Do you want to work for a local family-run company? Is a charity with a strong purpose you believe in on your wish list, or are large corporates more your thing?

For this exercise, it's also good to think about your values, a concept Lizzie Martin, Founder of Work Life Mother, is a huge advocate of for career success and fulfilment. For example, are you a teetotal person who saw a family member become an alcoholic; therefore, a brewery would be a no-go? Maybe you're a vegan and couldn't stand the thought of working for McDonald's. Do you get frustrated when your ideas aren't heard, so you want to work somewhere with open and transparent lines of communication, where all employees are encouraged to have a voice? Reflecting on what frustrates you or makes you restless can reveal a value that isn't being met. This self-awareness was crucial in Lizzie's decision to transition from a stable job to starting her own business. As Lizzie explains:[5]

'I started Work Life Mother not for the money or the flexibility, but because I knew what my personal values were. But values are not something people usually start to consider until they hit mid-career and start to evaluate their career direction and reflect on what it is that they want. Values are what motivate and drive you. They are ingredients that make you feel fulfilled in your life, in your relationships, and in your work. And you don't get to choose your values. They are not like your beliefs, which you can shape and influence. Your values are much more your DNA. They are what you have from a very young age and influence what fulfils or frustrates you.

One interesting question to ask if you want to discover your values is, "What really winds me up?" "What frustrates me?" and "What am I really restless about?" These questions indicate that one of your values isn't being met.

And that was the thing for me – it made me realise that I wanted to move out of that secure, stable place and do something different.'

For many, the transition to entrepreneurship is driven by flexibility or financial security. However, Lizzie's journey shows us that aligning your career with your values can be a more profound motivator to finding real job fulfilment.

Jen Smollett, a leadership and authenticity coach, is also a big fan of identifying your values to build your resilience and happiness at work. According to Jen:[6]

> 'Understanding your core values is crucial for leaders because they are the guiding principles that shape your leadership style and decision-making process. They provide clarity on what drives you, what you stand for, and what you expect from yourself and others. Core values lead to authentic, purposeful leadership, building trust and respect within your team. They guide you through challenges and tough decisions, bringing a sense of consistency and integrity in your actions.
>
> The best way to identify your values is to think about times when you have been at your absolute best. And when you've been at your best, this means you've been aligned with your values. So, think of two times when you've been at your absolute best. And then think of two times when you've been really frustrated by a situation. Usually, the frustration is because your value isn't there.'

So, what frustrates you? What winds you up? And what type of life would make you feel motivated and fulfilled? Write some ideas in the box here:

Lizzie also highlights the importance of resilience. Whether it's dealing with societal pressures or the challenges of entrepreneurship, finding strength in your values and decisions is crucial.

Great work! You should now have a list of potential jobs, companies, industries and values. This is a great basis for tailoring your CV and job search.

But before you dive into those job boards, take a minute to define YOUR version of success. Lizzie believes that knowing what success looks like to YOU is a good starting block when designing your dream career, because then you can plan how it looks and work around that. If you don't know what you are aiming for, you won't be in the driving seat. You'll find yourself being pulled and pushed in different directions, responding to what others think you should be doing rather than being true to yourself.

Everybody will have their own vision of what success looks like. Each vision will be different – and that's okay! It's important not to compare your career path to others. Comparisonitis is the first step to feeling disappointed in your life – remember, everyone always puts the best bits of their life on social media – no one's life really lives up to the hype. Comparing yourself to others' perceived success will only lead to feelings of inadequacy – even if you don't want their life anyway.

As well as knowing your values and definitions of success, Lizzie also recommends identifying your non-negotiables and setting those all-important boundaries. Again, this will help you identify suitable jobs (more on this in Chapter 2).

A boundary for you may be that you want to work school hours so you can pick up the kids every day, a job that doesn't have a commute longer than an hour, or travel no more than twice a month. Think – what does your life look like now? What are your career aspirations? What firm boundaries do you need to make this work? What can you flex?

How to Identify Suitable Jobs

So you know your strengths, values, definition of success and boundaries. This is a great foundation for identifying your ideal job. Based on this information, think about what types of jobs will tick your boxes. Get some input from friends and family – after all, these people know you best. Or speak to an impartial career advisor or careers coach, as they may have a unique perspective on what will suit you – and how to get there.

Look back on your previous work experience – what transferable skills will be useful in your dream career? For example, you may have worked as an estate agent and want to go into accounts management – all your relationship-building skills will be useful in your next career. Or perhaps you worked as an accountant but want to move to project management – any budgeting experience would be of use in project management when you are keeping on top of project budgets!

Now for your next to-do: brainstorm as many jobs as you can think of that would complement your personality whilst lighting you up – and find people who are doing those jobs to learn more about the positions and if they are right for you.

You can connect with people on LinkedIn or at your local university or college – many people are happy to chat and answer questions. Being curious is one of the best skills you can have. There's no such thing as a stupid question. What was their background before they got the job? What do they like about their position? What are the skills and attributes needed in the position? You can then compare their responses with your individual assessment of your strengths, values, measure of success, and career history – to see if those are the roles for you and adjust your job search accordingly.

As we close this chapter, remember that discovering your true career path involves self-reflection, resilience, and embracing your unique strengths and values. Whether you're reigniting your career, shifting paths, or stepping into the world of entrepreneurship, each step, however small, is a step towards a fulfilling and successful career. Your journey may not be linear or free from challenges, but armed with a clearer understanding of what drives you, and by setting boundaries that respect your personal and professional needs, you're well equipped to navigate the complexities of the working world. Remember, your career is not just a race to the finish line; it's a marathon that evolves with you. So, take a deep breath, embrace your journey with both its challenges and triumphs, and step forward with the knowledge that you have the tools within you to create a career that's not only successful but also a true reflection of who you are. Here's to your next chapter, where your newfound clarity and goals will lead you to uncharted, exciting paths!

Summary

Identify Your Strengths: Utilise tools like the Gallup strengths finder to understand your innate talents and use those to guide your career decisions. Recognising and leveraging your strengths can lead to more fulfilment and success.

Embrace Your Unique Qualities: Acknowledge that your unique personality traits have been with you since childhood. Instead of focusing on improving weaknesses, lean into your strengths for a more satisfying – and successful – career.

Reflect on Your Values: Consider what truly motivates and fulfils you, both in life and work. Identifying your core values, such as what frustrates you or brings you joy, can help clarify your career goals and choices.

Set Clear Career Goals: Based on your strengths and values, define what success looks like for you. Avoid comparing your journey to others and focus on setting personal and professional boundaries that align with YOUR aspirations.

Notes

1. Gallup (2020). *Now, Discover your Strengths: The revolutionary Gallup program that shows you how to develop your unique talents and strengths* (20th anniversary edition). Gallup Press.

2. Elizabeth Willetts (2024). From Self-Awareness to Success: Mastering Influence at Work with Roz Hobley. *Work It Like A Mum* (podcast) 7 March 2024. mp3 audio, 39:12, www.buzzsprout.com/2046830/14624517. Accessed 1 August 2024.

3. Steven Bartlett (2023). *The Diary of a CEO: The 33 Laws of Business and Life*. Portfolio.

4. Elizabeth Willetts (2024). From Self-Awareness to Success: Mastering Influence at Work with Roz Hobley. *Work It Like A Mum* (podcast) 7 March 2024. mp3 audio, 39:12, www.buzzsprout.com/2046830/14624517. Accessed 1 August 2024.

5. Elizabeth Willetts (2024). How to Discover & Stand By Your Values And Why It's Essential for Leading a Happier Life, With Return to Work Expert, Lizzie Martin. *Work It Like A Mum* (podcast) 23 March 2023. mp3 audio, 43:23, www.buzzsprout.com/2046830/12475044. Accessed 1 August 2024.

6. Investing in Women (2024). How to Be a Resilient Leader – Whatever Challenge Is Thrown At You. investinginwomen.co.uk/authentic-leadership-resilience-jen-smollett. Accessed 1 August 2024.

Chapter 2

What to Do When You Want to Switch Careers

In this chapter, I'm going to show you exactly how to pivot careers if you've realised you're not quite on the career path that lights you up. We'll dive into how to assess whether your current job is a good fit, explore the clever tactic of skill stacking to ramp up your career game, and map out how to smoothly transition into a new role that's not just about the money but is genuinely fulfilling. Whether you're eyeing a small shift or a total career makeover, I've got you covered with smart strategies and real-life stories to get you moving in the right direction. Let's figure this out together and get you on a path that feels right.

Some of you, after completing your inner work, will have had a light-bulb moment and realised you're in a job or career that actually does suit you, your personality and your values, in which case – well done, you can continue to build on existing skills and strengths with the aim (if it is one of your values) of climbing the career ladder. You can do this in the form of skill stacking, which I'll explain in more detail below.

But for others, you may have realised you are in the completely wrong job for you and your personality, and it now makes sense why you hate your job so much. Stick around because later in this chapter, I'll help you figure out how you can successfully pivot your career into something you love.

According to Alex Hormozi, a multi-millionaire, skill stacking and acquisition are the greatest investments you can make in your life.

But what is skill stacking? Hormozi often uses the example of the rapper Jay Z as someone who is an expert at skill stacking. For example, first, Jay Z had an ear for music and was a musician. Then, he learnt how to play beats before teaching himself how to rap and promote himself. Once he became an expert at making rap music and effectively promoting himself, he created a label where he learnt how to promote other people. Once all those skills were stacked, that skill stack was completely unique to Jay Z and he had ten times his previous revenue potential.[1] And it is this skill stacking that has enabled Jay Z to amass a net worth of $2 billion whilst Eminem, who has stuck primarily to rapping, is worth a mere $250 million.[2]

To bring that example to everyday life, imagine you're an expert at making personal TikToks. You learn how the platform works and offer to make TikToks for friends and acquaintances, growing their social media following. You then learn how some of the other social media platforms work. You grow your presence on those before deciding to become a freelancer offering social media support to businesses. You help to grow other people's businesses whilst effectively promoting yourself and your services and become more in demand, so hire an associate to help with the workload. Your workload increases, so you hire another associate, and before long, you have created a social media agency. You then learn about other forms of digital marketing, mastering paid adverts and email marketing. Now you have a digital marketing agency. You then get asked to help a client organise in-person events and do their PR. Until eventually, you have created a multi-million-pound marketing agency unique to you and your talents that started from a single TikTok video.

Or here's an example if you are employed: you join a company as their social media coordinator and learn your craft – what works and doesn't – until you are no longer just posting the content on behalf of someone else but strategising what content to put and where. You then put your hand up to learn how to run paid ads. You go on a course and, again, over time, master the art of digital ads. You now have a good reputation as someone creative, trustworthy and reliable. You volunteer for additional projects and promotions, learning SEO and email marketing whilst honing your management skills, until you eventually run the digital marketing department. You work closely with other marketing departments – learn what they do, take additional courses, and offer to help, and when a promotion becomes available for a Head of Marketing role, you are in a strong position to apply for it because you have continued to develop your skills and experience in your niche, and your talents are hugely valuable to your employer.

If one of your values is money-related, you can transfer your skills to the higher-paying legal or financial services industries. And then boom – you've reached the top of your career in a high-paying industry and are well renumerated for it.

But what if you don't feel you're on the right career path? Perhaps you have an inkling to try something you've always wanted to try but never felt brave enough, and you have played it safe in a job that you were perhaps pushed into by parental pressure or because it pays the bills.

You might know you have more to give, want a more purpose-driven role, or would love the opportunity to move into a completely new field. But rather than spray and pray, as so many applicants do when they apply for multiple roles that they appear to have no relevant experience for (at least to the recruiter reviewing the CVs), you will need to consider your application at a much deeper level.

Roz Hobley, one of the UK's leading leadership and performances coaches, is an expert on how to build credibility at work. When applying for new roles, she says that the candidates most likely to be selected for interview are those who have demonstrated their *relevance* to the role. Therefore, when applying for any role, you need to look at the job advert, candidate specification, and your background, and highlight to the hiring manager and recruiter how your experience is relevant to the role through tailored CVs and cover letters.

As Roz[3] says, 'Being seen as credible is crucial when applying for a job. And being credible is about being relevant. When preparing for a job interview, it's about taking your personality, skills, experience, knowledge, and network and having the ability to make them relevant to the person interviewing you – showing that you understand and are relevant to their world, to their context, to their challenges.'

I coach many individuals who want to completely switch careers and want to land their dream job straight away – without putting the work in first. Remember, no one owes you a job. Employers want to hire people they know will be able to add value from the start! You've got to be realistic – you will be competing with candidates who have potentially spent years working in that industry and honing their craft. What I advise them – and what I'll advise you – is that if you want to do a complete 180-degree turn in your career, view your dream job as a destination you will reach in perhaps five years – and the next couple of jobs as stepping stones to get there. What jobs that are not a million miles from your current one, but closer to your ideal job, will give you the transferable skills and experience you need – and make you a more attractive candidate to that employer? Once you've identified them, start applying, and once in a stepping-stone role, use the time to stack the skills you need for your dream job. As the saying goes – good things come to those who wait. For example, you may be a teacher who wants to become a fashion designer. Can you use your teaching experience to get a job in learning and development in a fashion house, take a design course in the evening, put your hand up to volunteer for the design department leading up to fashion shows, gain that all-important relevant experience, and make internal sideways moves from there?

Don't be afraid to retrain if needed, whether it be going back to college, doing an apprenticeship, or taking an online course. Retraining can give you the chance to do a complete 180-degree pivot and move into something new. Your local college will have a prospectus of the courses available, the time commitment, what qualifications you will gain, and the career prospects available at the end of your course so you can decide if this is right for you.

A word of warning – if you want to do a complete 180-degree turn and move into a completely different field, be prepared to start again at the bottom of the ladder as you will be competing with candidates having potentially years of relevant experience if you're looking to stay at the same level you are currently on. If you can't take the financial hit of a huge salary cut, could you reduce the hours you spend in your current role whilst building up your experience in your new field? Or can you start a side hustle (and see Chapter 19, 'Starting Your Own Business') in the evenings that will support you financially? Where there is a will, there is always a way, but making such a big leap will require some creative thinking.

Case Study – Jodie Mason, Brand, Digital and Communications Executive at Saint-Gobain

Jodie Mason works in internal communications at Saint-Gobain, one of the world's largest construction companies. But her career with them didn't start in communications or even marketing. No, in fact, when Jodie originally joined Saint-Gobain in 2015, she joined their credit services team. Jodie has made an art form of continuing to move sideways whilst working for a large company that can offer internal opportunities and the security of a regular paycheck while figuring out where she eventually wanted to be. From credit services, Jodie put up her hand for an internal move and moved to reception, which sat in workspace services, where she again put up her hand and got a promotion to eventually lead their facilities management team. During the COVID pandemic, Jodie had a taste of internal communications when she was very involved with creating resources for colleagues to support making their workspaces COVID safe. In doing so, Jodie realised that internal communications was something she really enjoyed and started hankering for a permanent role in this area.

Jodie has become adept at the internal networking so many of us need to thrive in an organisation, so when she heard about a role in internal communications, she raised her hand again and sought out the manager of the team, told them she was interested in the role, and was able to demonstrate the relevance of her previous experience and transferable skills to the position. She was subsequently offered the position of Brand, Digital and Communications Executive – a role she loves. She's now in the position of being able to pursue further learning within communications or explore further lateral moves into marketing or HR-related functions – a far cry from her original start in the credit services team!

Jodie's career is a masterclass in leveraging a broad skill set for professional growth, and her story is a powerful reminder that career progression isn't just about climbing upwards – it's about moving in whichever direction brings growth, fulfilment, and opportunity. With each move, Jodie gathered a wealth of experience, transforming every role into a stepping stone towards her current success as a key player in Saint-Gobain's communications team. Her journey demonstrates that sometimes, the best way forward is to move sideways, explore new fields, and redefine what success and happiness mean to you.

As Jodie explains:[4]

'Many people view progress as up, up, up, but actually, it could be sideways, down, diagonal. My career path so far has been credit services, sideways into accounts, diagonally into customer services, and then back down again.

I think it's really eclectic. But it's really easy to feel that if you're not going up, then you can't be progressing. But actually, all of these different experiences gave me all sorts of skills. And if you start looking at yourself as a collection of skills and strengths rather than a set of qualifications – or "I currently do this, so I must only be able to do this" – if you look at yourself differently and value yourself differently, and then tell people about your skill set – and explain that value in a way that they can see, it becomes much easier to make those connections and think about what you **could do**, *rather than what you feel like you have to do.'*

Jodie is not the only one who found that making a sideways move positively impacted her career. When Rachel Exton, a VP in Marketing, was told her flexible working request would only be granted if she took a less senior role in another department, she almost turned her employer down, but it turned out to be the best thing she ever did. Here are Rachel's thoughts on the benefits of sideways moves:[5]

'I did contemplate not going back, but I love work, and I love what I do. And starting at a brand new employer with two young kids is really difficult. I'd been with my employer for ten years. I knew the people. I knew the company. I had a really strong support network and reputation. So, after a lot of soul-searching and some great conversations with people, I decided to do it.

It was something completely different. It was outside of marketing – it was actually working in retail. I'd never done retail before, but you know what? It turned into something for which I am forever grateful. And I would absolutely advocate now to anybody, whether you're a working mum or not, to think about developing your career sideways, as well as going up. What I learned in the 18 months that I did the role were skills I would have never acquired if I'd stayed in marketing and just been focused on going up that tree. It made me become so much more rounded in terms of my skill base, but also my leadership style. And for me, when I was ready to return to marketing after 18 months I could say, 'I'm ready to increase my days now and look at what more I can bring'. I'm much more rounded and have learned so much more than if I just stayed in marketing. I would have never normally done it because I was so set on going upwards, but now I would recommend it to anybody.'

And if you do want to climb to the top of you career tree, you will need to embrace the idea of sideways rather than always upwards moves to advance your career. A CEO of a company needs to have a broad understanding of how a business works, rather than just his or her section. And it's only by working across a business that you will develop this commercial knowledge and understanding, which will make you a truly great leader who can take your business to new heights.

Navigating a career change or re-evaluating your current career path can feel like standing at a crossroads, unsure of which direction to take. Whether you're skill stacking in your current role or considering an exciting leap into a completely different field, it's all about strategy and ensuring each move aligns with your values. If you treat each career move like a chess piece, thoughtfully advancing towards your ultimate goal, you'll ensure that you're not just chasing a paycheck but building a career that's genuinely fulfilling and lights you up. Don't just dream about a satisfying career – strategically build one.

Summary

Embrace Skill Stacking: Understand that accumulating and combining diverse skills can significantly enhance your career potential. Drawing inspiration from figures like Jay Z and everyday examples, learn how skill stacking can create unique career paths and opportunities for growth.

Evaluate Your Current Position: Reflect on whether your current job aligns with your strengths, personality, and values. If it does, consider how you can further develop your skills within this role. If not, recognise the possibility of pursuing a career more aligned with your real interests.

Strategic Career Moves: Discover the power of lateral moves within your career to gain broader experience and skill sets. Case studies like Jodie Mason's illustrate how moving sideways or even taking a step back can ultimately propel your career forward by diversifying your skills and experiences.

Navigating Career Transitions: For those considering a major career change, understand the importance of making your past experiences relevant to your new field. Tailor your applications to highlight how your unique background makes you a valuable candidate, and be open to retraining or starting at a lower level to achieve your dream career.

Notes

1. BizNinja (2023). Alex Hormozi Breaks Down Talent Stacking in 8 Minutes: 'The Greatest Investment You Can Make!' YouTube. www.youtube.com/watch?v=IOW6y9z5lYU. Accessed 1 August 2024.
2. Graham Falk (2024). Who is the richest musician in the world 2024? Top 11 richest rappers in the world, Eminem, P-Diddy net worth. *The Scotsman*. www.scotsman.com/arts-and-culture/music/who-is-the-richest-rapper-in-the-world-2024-richest-rap-stars-in-the-world-jay-z-eminem-p-diddy-snoop-dogg-net-worth-4527778?page=1. Accessed 1 August 2024.
3. Elizabeth Willetts (2024). From Self-Awareness to Success: Mastering Influence at Work with Roz Hobley. *Work It Like A Mum* (podcast) 7 March 2024. mp3 audio, 39:12, www.buzzsprout.com/2046830/14624517. Accessed 1 August 2024.
4. Elizabeth Willetts (2024). Sideways, Down, and Diagonal: Redefining Career Success and the Art of the Career Pivot. *Work It Like A Mum* (podcast) 29 February 2024. mp3 audio, 39:06, www.buzzsprout.com/2046830/14579117. Accessed 1 August 2024.
5. Elizabeth Willetts (2024). Can You Really Have It All? Debunking Career Myths with Rachel Exton. *Work It Like A Mum* (podcast) 2 May 2024. mp3 audio, 46:44, www.buzzsprout.com/2046830/14992698-can-you-really-have-it-all-debunking-career-myths-with-rachel-exton. Accessed 1 August 2024.

Chapter 3

Where to Look for Jobs

$\mathbf{F}$inding a job often feels like a full-time job itself. Searching the job boards for your dream job can feel like looking for a needle in a haystack – and that's before we've got to lengthy application forms, tailoring your CV, writing those cover letters, and preparing for interviews (don't worry – I've got you covered on these in later chapters).

But in this chapter, we'll cover the obvious and not-so-obvious places you can search for roles and help you unearth that hidden gem.

Your Existing Company

Yes – that's right: as Jodie Mason has demonstrated in the previous chapter, your existing company may be able to offer you your dream career – and lots of interesting roles to develop and stretch you. Most companies won't want to lose someone they've spent months (and possibly years) training – someone who knows them, their culture, processes and quirks. They would rather keep you – even if it means in a different role (and therefore some additional training) because they know you're trustworthy, can learn quickly, and will be a good company and culture fit. In fact, most large companies have internal careers pages on their intranet dedicated to promoting internal mobility. You'll be able to search for job openings within your firm before they're opened up to the external market (see how much they want to retain their existing staff there!). The good news is, the interview process is a lot less intensive for internal movements – hopefully, you'll have just the one round to meet your new hiring manager, and you're done. And if you really impress in your existing role, you may find yourself regularly 'being tapped up' (approached) by the other managers in your company, begging you to join their teams – always a great confidence boost.

It's polite to give your existing manager a heads-up that you're hoping to make an internal move – explaining what you're hoping to do and why. A good manager will have your best interests at heart and be personally targeted on how much they do to develop their team, so they should be able to keep an eye out for you too, or put in a good word with your potential new manager.

Job Boards

Depending on your specialism, you could look on niche job boards such as eFinancialCareers (for those looking for a new job in financial services), TES (if you want a job in education), or my job board (Investing in Women) if you're looking for a flexible/part-time job. There are thousands of specialist job boards, so if you type your niche plus job board into Google, some of the most popular job boards will appear.

In addition to the niche sites, it is also worth visiting the bigger, more broader job boards that list thousands of jobs, such as Indeed, Reed, or Monster Jobs.

Once on the job board, you can search for the job title you're targeting and your location in the search bar. Then, scroll down the listings and apply to any that take your fancy. Job adverts on these sites can receive hundreds of applications, so a cover letter explaining your relevance to the role and interest in the position will help your application stand out.

Recruitment Agencies

Now, I know recruitment agents are down there with estate agents in professions that are in it for themselves, but if you find a good recruitment agent, they're worth their weight in gold. Not only will they actively contact you about suitable roles as they're added to 'their books' (and many time-pressed employers won't use job boards to advertise their roles – particularly for senior positions), but they will also market you to their clients if they feel you have the right skill set and personality. A recruitment agency will help perfect your CV, coach you through interviews, and advise you on job offers, all for FREE (the employer pays them when they successfully hire someone). And if you pick a good one who stays in the same industry as you, you could literally work with them on and off for years – every time you want to change roles, in fact.

LinkedIn Is Your Friend

LinkedIn is the number one social media platform for candidates and recruiters alike. Recruiters regularly search LinkedIn to find suitable candidates for the roles they're hiring for, meaning your dream job might literally drop into your inbox. Therefore, it's imperative that you're not only on LinkedIn but that you have a well-optimised profile and a relevant network so you're found by the right people (i.e. the hiring managers and recruiters hiring for your dream job). Check out Chapter 9 for the inside scoop on how to write a LinkedIn profile recruiters will LOVE, build a network and get noticed on one of the fastest-growing social media platforms. As well as writing a well-optimised profile, you can also write a post on LinkedIn specifying that you are 'open to work' (in fact, LinkedIn even has an 'open to work' green banner you can add to your profile picture that tells recruiters just that – that you're open to work and therefore an active candidate to contact). But back to your 'open to work' social media post – don't forget to add what roles you're looking for and your relevant skills and experience. You'll be astonished just how supportive your LinkedIn connections will be – often, those posts go far and wide on the platform, jobs will be suggested to you in the comments – and your next hiring manager may just reach out directly with your dream job straight to your inbox – I mean, just how cool is that?!?

Facebook Groups can be Hidden Gems

Your local area will most certainly have a Facebook group dedicated to local jobs. Type '"your town" jobs' into the Facebook search bar, and a list of groups you can join should appear. Click join, wait to be approved, then scroll through recent listings to see if any take your fancy. Details on how to apply should be included in the post. Like LinkedIn, you can write an 'open to work' post for the group, then sit back and watch social media work its magic.

Network, Network, Network

According to *Business Insider*, employers fill 70% of job vacancies before even advertising them. Using your network when job searching is essential to avoid missing out on the 'hidden job market'.

Let friends, family and ex-colleagues know you are looking for work. Ask them to listen out for you. They might be able to recommend you to an employer (or their employer) who is hiring. Tell everyone you meet that you're looking for work! Make and nurture contacts on and offline, as you never know where your dream job may be hiding – and who can help you find it.

Armed with these tips, you're well on your way to finding your perfect job – and the next few chapters are full of advice on how to get it.

Summary

Explore Internal Opportunities: Don't overlook the potential for career growth within your current organisation. Internal moves can offer valuable new experiences and growth without the need to start over elsewhere.

Utilise Specialised Job Boards and Recruitment Agencies: Niche job boards and reputable recruitment agencies can be invaluable resources, offering access to targeted job opportunities and professional guidance throughout the job search process.

Maximise Your LinkedIn Presence: Ensure your LinkedIn profile is optimised to attract the attention of recruiters and hiring managers. A strong LinkedIn presence can lead to amazing job opportunities falling right into your inbox!

Tap into the Hidden Job Market: Remember that many jobs are never advertised publicly. Leverage your personal and professional networks, including social media groups and offline connections, to uncover these hidden opportunities.

Chapter 4

Career Breaks

Now, first things first – repeat after me – a career break is not a career killer. You're probably more conscious of your career break and the dates you've been out of work than anyone else. I find that people place lots of emphasis and negative feelings towards even a short career break of a couple of years (and sometimes even months!). You're working for a long time – roughly 40+ years. Therefore, a couple of years out of the workforce to do something else is a short period of time in the grand scheme of things.

Remember – lots of people take career breaks during their working lives. Perhaps you have taken time out to look after young children or an elderly relative. Maybe you needed a break for health reasons, took a gap year to travel the world, spent time volunteering, or were made redundant. Whatever your reasons, career breaks are increasingly common in our modern working world. And there's no such thing as a job for life!

Tiggy McCool is now a partner at management consultancy Nine Feet Tall. She's had several career breaks and here's what she has to say:[1]

> *'In terms of career breaks, I've had a few, so I feel I am an experienced hand in this area! The first was due to redundancy when I was 28. So it wasn't a choice. At the time, I was initially a bit shocked, but once I had had the opportunity to digest the news and think about my options, I decided to use my redundancy payout to turn lemons into lemonade and go travelling around*

the world. Despite concern from others about the risk and impact on my career and whether I would be able to find another job, this decision had a hugely positive impact. It helped me to focus on what type of work I wanted to do and what my next step in the career ladder could be. It freed up my thinking. Without that chance to reflect and make a change, my career would have looked very different today.

When I returned, I took a contract role, as I knew I wanted to have a family and maximise my income before taking any maternity leave. Some friends thought not returning to a permanent role was a bit risky, but I knew plenty of project work was available, so I took a leap of faith and worked for myself for several years before I had my first son. When he arrived, we talked about how long I would stay at home. Ultimately, I decided to take three years to be home with my son, which felt like a long time. After the first year, I was worried about the perception of being a stay-at-home mum and whether others would view me as not being ambitious. But I spoke to many friends who had gone back to work quickly, and they were finding it hard to juggle, so I started to realise that whatever we choose to do, there's a natural tendency to compare ourselves to others and to feel a degree of 'mum guilt' rather than enjoying the now. When I started to think about my next move, the culture and purpose of the company I was going to work for had become really important to me. It had to be something special to be worth being away from my child. I started a new role, which I loved, and a few years later, I had my daughter, Kitty. Six months into my planned maternity leave, my husband was made redundant, and I had to return to work at short notice. My employer was super flexible and welcomed an honest conversation about what I needed, so I returned to work part-time. Five years later, I had my youngest boy, Sam, and chose to stay at home for nine precious months with him, but then I wanted to return to work. Again, I talked with my employer about what a phased return could look like, which helped me transition back into working life.

This time at home has not set me back in any way at all. I just think there's a bit of a myth that taking time out of work will have some detrimental effect on your career.

I've found that it's given me a lot of clarity on what I really want out of life and work. Some people's careers can span 40+ years. It's a heck of a long time. I heartily believe if you get the opportunity to go and do something different, then, as long as you can afford to do it, go ahead and try it because we're working for a long time. Employers' attitudes towards gaps in CVs and career breaks have also evolved, so it is easier to explain your life choices. If the employer doesn't understand, then perhaps they are not the right choice for you.

Hindsight is a wonderful thing, of course. It can feel like you're taking a long time out at the time, but when you look back on it, it's so short in terms of your total working life. Having a few more months at home and being ready to return is really important for how you feel about yourself and your role as a mum, and whether you feel mentally and emotionally prepared and excited to be back at work. Because there's nothing worse than being at work when you feel guilty about it. I just think the whole conversation about a return to work and when the right time is, is something employers could be a lot better at. Be open to these conversations and encourage them.

When I was back at work and my husband was at home with the children, I was worried that people would think I didn't care about my kids. The concept of "mum guilt", which I've talked to a lot of friends about, is really common. When I first went back to work full time, my husband was one of the only dads regularly in the playground doing pick-ups and drop-offs. He found it difficult, too. Thankfully, dads doing the school run is now much more common, partly due to COVID and the rise in flexible and hybrid working. Now, my son is 16, and there's a lot more variety in working patterns. I think the pandemic has meant parenting is no longer viewed as a sole parent's responsibility but instead a shared one, which is absolutely right. Parenting doesn't stop at 9 a.m. and restart at 5 p.m. – and many employers have moved their thinking forward.'

So there you are – lose the guilt. Do what's right for you and embrace those career breaks! Now that we've cleared that one up, here are some tips for returning to work from a career break like a pro.

What do YOU Want?

Before jumping straight into your job search, a return after a career break offers you the perfect opportunity to take some time to think about what you want. You may have changed during your time away. Your goals and priorities may have altered. Maybe you fancy a career change – a career break provides the perfect opportunity to make a switch. What hours do you need, what salary, and, perhaps most importantly, what do you enjoy doing and are good at? Returning to work after a career break is the perfect time for you to implement the tips and advice we covered in Chapter 1 about how to identify your strengths, values and measures of success.

Make sure you use this time to also reflect on your career break. Did you learn any new skills? Spend time volunteering? Take courses or even start a side hustle? Whatever you spent your career break doing, you'll have developed new skills and perspectives that will be transferable back into paid employment – some of which will be worth mentioning on your CV or at an interview. Employers want to hire proactive people. Showing you continued developing skills, whether at home watching relevant YouTube tutorials or more formally at an adult education centre, highlights your motivation and enthusiasm.

Do Your Research

If you want to return to your previous industry or career – particularly if it's competitive or fast-paced, then you'll need to spend time brushing up on any developments that happened in your absence. Consider a refresher or short course to demonstrate your commitment and ensure you are up to date. Also, ensure any memberships are current and you've read any recent publications or news updates. If you can demonstrate that you've kept up to date on industry developments and taken time to brush up your skills and knowledge, you'll be seen as a more valuable and attractive hire than someone who hasn't.

Many large companies now offer return-to-work schemes. These are similar to graduate schemes in that they provide a structured programme that allows you to learn and develop whilst being paid on the job. Many return-to-work schemes also offer part-time hours. It's great if you have other commitments, so it's worth looking to see what is on offer from the big employers in your industry.

Network, Network, Network

Don't forget to use your existing connections when searching for a job. Spend time reaching out to ex-colleagues, clients, friends, and family members and let them know you are searching for a new role. Studies show that at least 70% of jobs are never advertised, so don't be afraid of putting yourself out there to tap into this hidden market. Please refer to my advice in Chapter 10 for how to do this effectively and make the most of these opportunities.

Make the Most of Your Online Presence

If you are a job seeker, you need to be on LinkedIn. With over 1 billion users (at the time of writing), it is the largest professional social networking platform globally and THE social media network of choice for recruiters and employers. And, with an optimised keyword-rich LinkedIn profile, future employers can find and approach you for their vacancies. To make the most of the platform and increase your chances of being found and hired for your dream job, read Chapter 9, which is dedicated to helping you create a recruiter-friendly profile and use the platform to build your network effectively.

Be prepared to discuss your career break if asked during the interview. If you don't mention it, it can be the elephant in the room. Be clear about your reasons for taking a career break and what skills you learned and developed, but don't overdo it. As I mentioned earlier, you're more than your career break – it doesn't define you. For more interview tips, read Chapter 11, which covers how to interview well in more detail.

Update Your CV to Reflect Your Career Break

Don't try to hide your career break. Lying about dates will always come back to haunt you, and employers will often make (the wrong) assumptions. You are more than your career break; you don't need to 'over-explain' your time away.

Personally, I don't think you necessarily need to include a career break on a CV, as it actually draws more attention to it. An interviewer can always question you about a gap in your CV during an interview if they want to. But if you do want to include it, writing the following (or similar, depending on your circumstances) will suffice:

May 2018–September 2021

Career break raising my young family

Also, putting dates to the right of the page like this:

May 2018–September 2021

makes them less visible because we read left to right and tend to focus more on things on the left of the page.

Practice Interviewing

It's natural to be nervous if you haven't had a job interview in a while. Spend some time practising interviewing. Ask a friend or family member to be a mock interviewer and ask some interview questions. Practising your answers will help you feel more confident. You could also record answers to some common interview questions on your phone, play them back, and think about how to improve.

Everyone Is on Their Own Path

It can be hard not to compare yourself to others, but we're all on our own career ladder – one that we climb at our own pace depending on who we are, what we want, and what else is happening in our lives. Try to stay in your lane rather than comparing yourself to others. And know your worth! You're a fabulous, conscientious, hard-working individual who will be a real asset to your next employer.

And, remember, if a potential employer can't appreciate that you have a life outside the workplace, is that the type of place you'd like to work anyway?

Case Study – Christa Davis, Mechanical Engineer at UKAEA

Christa Davis is a mechanical engineer who had a 20-year career break to raise her children. Yes, 20 years before returning to her career at the UK Atomic Energy Authority on an engineering returnship. Like Tiggy, Christa took time out to spend with her young family. With three small boys, life was hectic and about 10 years into her career break, Christa started thinking about returning to work. Here is her experience:[2]

'Before I knew it, I'd been out of the job scene for ten years. It was always my intention to get back to my career. It just didn't seem to happen – there wasn't the time to fit in. And then, before I knew it, when it was time to start thinking about work again… time had moved on.

And I realised I'd had a massive career break and felt rather out of date and out of touch with what had happened and how technology had advanced in those years. I wasn't fully confident about returning to an engineering career, so I started looking for available training opportunities. The Royal Aeronautical Society was operating a scheme that gave bursaries to engineers wanting to study for a master's degree. They'd seen a shortage of higher qualified engineers and wanted to encourage more engineers to study further. They offered bursaries, and I managed to get one of those and signed up for a part-time master's degree in aerospace.

It reassured me that I hadn't completely lost all of my maths and science skills in those ten years at home with the kids and that I could keep up with the other students. It also gave me some extra background and more up-to-date technical information I'd missed out on over the years.

At the same time, I obtained part-time work doing admin and reception to earn some more money to cover the rest of the course fees and extra expenses. A little extra money is always good when you've got three kids.

I received my master's degree in November 2019. It took me five years, studying part-time. But then, obviously, in February 2020, COVID struck. So, all my good intentions to start applying for new jobs and get back into the job market were turned on their heads. Aircraft were not flying because no one was allowed to go on holiday. Companies were making their engineers redundant. It seemed the worst time to be looking for a new aeronautical or aircraft engineering job. But COVID didn't go on forever, did it? And COVID did change the way we work so much. Although it seemed disastrous timing that I was newly qualified just as COVID struck, it's changed how we can work with hybrid and remote working becoming normal. And actually, my choice of jobs was much broader after the pandemic because I didn't have to restrict myself to extremely local jobs that would fit into family life. I could broaden my mileage range. I looked at companies all over the UK offering remote or hybrid working. Having the option not to commute every day just makes life so much easier.

But even with my master's degree and being more newly qualified, the fact that I had a huge career gap on my CV meant I didn't look like a typical engineering candidate. So I had lots of rejections. But finally, I had an offer from the UK Atomic Energy Authority (UKAEA). I'd applied for an engineering post with them, and they came back to me and said, "Well, you don't quite fit the requirements for that post, but we are hoping to start up a new STEM returners scheme to hire people who have had a career break, or career change".

My return has been really positive. I've been surprised at how much engineering knowledge I still remember. Everyone's been so welcoming. The department that I've joined, RACE, does get a lot of new starters among the graduates it takes on. They also take on summer placement students and year-in-industry students. They're used to lots of new people starting. Therefore, it offers a comprehensive programme to help people train and settle in.

So, I started the STEM returners scheme full-time on-site, five days a week for the first six weeks. That was my choice because I wanted to get the maximum out of the experience, get to know my colleagues, and build my network. It is so much easier to learn things if you can see them in front of you.

But now I'm just going in for team meetings, which tend to be once a week. I usually go in for that, with the rest of the time, working from home.

I realise now that engineering is my passion. You know, in school, what you're good at. What lessons do you enjoy the most? And that tends to be how you choose your career without knowing what else exists. But having been out in the world and come back to it, it's sort of reaffirmed that, yes, this is, for me, brilliant.'

Summary

Your Career Break is Just a Chapter: Remember, your career break is just one chapter in your professional story, not the entire narrative. Focus on how this period has contributed to your growth rather than worrying about how it might be perceived. You're more conscious of the break than anyone else; most employers are interested in what you can bring to their team now.

Embrace Continuous Learning: Recognise that industries are constantly evolving, and continuous learning is key to adapting and thriving in your career. This mindset will not only make you more marketable but also build your confidence and enrich your professional journey and career with new challenges and opportunities for growth.

Stay Updated on Industry Trends: Use your career break as an opportunity to catch up on the latest developments in your field. Consider enrolling in relevant courses, attending workshops, or obtaining certifications that can refresh your knowledge and skills, demonstrating to employers your commitment to staying current and proactive about your professional development.

Highlight Your Self-Awareness and Adaptability: Use your career break to showcase your self-awareness and adaptability to potential employers. Demonstrating that you've used this time to reassess your career goals, acquire new skills, and adapt to changes in your industry reflects positively on your character and professional resilience.

Notes

1. Elizabeth Willetts (2023). What Does the Future of Work Look Like? And Why a Career Break Is Not a Career Killer. With Management Consultant, Tiggy Atkinson. *Work It Like A Mum* (podcast) 23 February 2023. MP3 audio, 44:46, www.buzzsprout.com/2046830/12278742. Accessed 1 August 2024.
2. Elizabeth Willetts (2024). Brick by Brick: How Christa Davies Rebuilt Her Engineering Career After a 20-Year Career Break. *Work It Like A Mum* (podcast) 15 February 2024. MP3 audio, 38:14, www.buzzsprout .com/2046830/14489198-brick-by-brick-how-christa-davies-rebuilt-her-engineering-career-after-a-20-year-career-break. Accessed 1 August 2024.

Chapter 5

Staying Positive When Life Throws a Curveball

Life isn't predictable. There are highs and lows, twists and turns. Sometimes, the best-laid plans come unstuck, and your career can take a back seat in those moments. Certain events leave you with no option but to prioritise other parts of your life. Or sometimes, work provides a well-needed outlet when you feel your personal life is falling apart.

When I was battling infertility for four and a half years, my career was certainly not at the forefront of my mind. I spent every day feeling anxious, isolated and preoccupied. I lost all my confidence – certainly not the best ingredients for putting myself forward for promotions or trying to climb the career ladder. All my spare time was spent visiting Dr Google, trying to self-analyse why I couldn't have a baby or researching IVF clinics – it certainly wasn't spent upskilling professionally networking or taking on additional projects. And although I wasn't a bad performer at work, I probably wasn't the best employee either. I coasted career-wise during those years, treading water, viewing my job as something that could pay the bills and fund a possible IVF treatment. It certainly was not my priority. My priority was to get pregnant and have a baby. Work came a very far second.

But what my job did give me was somewhere to go and take my mind off my personal life. At work, I could be 'Corporate-Recruiter Liz' instead of 'sad Liz who couldn't get pregnant'. And having two babies eventually born in close succession meant I basically had two back-to-back maternity leaves. Throw in a pandemic, and I'd suddenly been out of work for three years.

And, like many women, I lost a lot of confidence during my time out of the workplace. I regularly questioned whether I could remember how to do my job, whether my skills were still needed, and if all my old colleagues and network would have forgotten who I was.

And you know what, I'm not going to lie, when I first launched my recruitment business, Investing in Women, it was hard. I felt nervous, exposed and like a big fat imposter for quite a while. But pretty soon, I realised I hadn't forgotten how to do my job – and my old friends and colleagues hadn't forgotten me either. And actually, time out of the workplace had given me more energy and motivation for my career; I now wanted to work and it provided me with a fresh outlet after being locked indoors during the pandemic. My experiences of infertility and parenting gave me a new perspective and empathy that I could bring to my role – great skills when I'm working so closely with people all the time.

I'm now grateful for that twist and turn that stalled my career during those years. I think it made me a better person – certainly better at doing my job and dealing with others, as I'm now always aware you never know what someone is going through behind closed doors. And actually, if you can be honest and open about your experiences, you'll soon realise no one goes through life completely unscathed – everyone's life includes those detours, twists and turns. If you accept that nothing is always perfect, the twists and turns can actually be the making of you and your career – or the start of a new, exciting chapter.

This chapter is a collection of stories from women who have overcome illness or are looking after children with additional needs but have managed to pick their careers back up, keep them going – or even been inspired to start something new. Their experiences and the skills and knowledge you've gained in the rest of this book will inspire you and give you the confidence to know that a catastrophic event in your personal life does not take away your professional skills and experience. Rather, it can give you a fresh perspective and new skills that will make you even better at your job. The following case studies highlight some experiences.

Case Study – Charlotte Ralph, Personal Stylist with Colour Me Beautiful

Charlotte Ralph was a regular mum – she had a toddler and a growing business as a Colour Me Beautiful personal stylist that she had recently decided to focus on full-time. Life was going well, but one night, everything changed when she discovered a lump in her neck during a date with her husband.[1]

'We'd been living in Fleet for about a year, and Ben was just approaching two. I was very busy all the time, either looking after him or working or just, you know, running the household. I didn't have much time to myself then. It was my birthday. My husband and I had gone out for a meal by ourselves, which was completely unheard of. At that point, I hadn't been feeling good. I'd had a really stiff neck, I hadn't been sleeping. I went off to the loo while we were in this Indian restaurant, and I was massaging my neck a bit because it felt so stiff, and I realised there was a lump in my neck. My blood just ran cold. I knew there was something very wrong. So I booked a GP appointment and went to see him. He also looked quite worried and referred me for an urgent scan. That period of waiting for the scan and then waiting for the results was one of the worst periods of my life.

But I had the scan. It looked suspicious, and they referred me for a biopsy. They could see lots of lumps in my neck. I was in a lot of pain; I was very tired, I was having night sweats, all these things which I kind of probably hadn't really noticed because I was a new mum and wasn't getting much sleep. So I just put it down to all that.'

Charlotte's biopsy confirmed her worst fears. She was diagnosed with Hodgkin's lymphoma just weeks after discovering she was pregnant again. The good news was that Charlotte was told she would be able to continue with the pregnancy but would have to postpone starting her chemotherapy treatment until the second trimester.

'So, the chemo was every two weeks. I'd spend a day at the hospital and then a good few days recovering. I was lucky I didn't have really awful side effects from the chemo. But I was also contending with the pregnancy, so I was tired. My mum and dad came up every other week when I was having the chemo to help out, which was amazing and much needed. I was just very tired. But the effects built up cumulatively, so towards the end of the pregnancy, as I was getting more heavily pregnant, I started to feel more unwell.

They induced the baby about three or four weeks early because my liver was struggling a bit, and they needed to get her out so that I could recover. But I'd also had a horrible feeling that chemo wasn't doing what it was meant to. I hadn't been able to have the normal scans that people would have to check whether the chemo was working because of the pregnancy. And I knew in the bottom of my heart that it hadn't worked, and I had a feeling that the scan after I'd had the baby probably wasn't going to be good news.'

Charlotte's hunch was right. The chemo hadn't worked. Although her cancer was meant to be treatable, Charlotte was in the low percentage of Hodgkin's lymphoma patients who didn't respond to initial treatment. What followed was another six years of treatments, visits to and from the hospital, and waiting for scans, tests, and new rounds of treatment and medication. Just before the COVID pandemic hit, Charlotte contracted what she was told was pneumonia and became very unwell.

'Somehow, I'd managed to cling to my life, but things were just getting more and more hopeless. Then, just before COVID, I had a nasty infection, and I was taken to the hospital. I remember being put on oxygen. The next thing I knew, I'd woken up. I had all these tubes attached to me, and I'd been in a coma for three weeks.

And they think now that I'd had a fungal type of pneumonia and they think I'd also had COVID, but it was before people had heard about COVID, so I'd been in intensive care on a ventilator for three weeks. They thought I wasn't going to make it.

When I woke up, I couldn't do anything. I'd lost all my muscles. I couldn't swallow. I had to learn to swallow again – to talk, walk, eat, and drink.'

Charlotte eventually went into full remission from her cancer thanks to the amazing generosity of an anonymous stem cell donor. Here's how Charlotte explains the process:

'So, you have this infusion, and the donor's immune system becomes your immune system, and it is capable of recognising cancer cells, which your immune system hasn't been able to do.'

And after a six-year ordeal, taking life on what felt like an hour-by-hour basis, Charlotte was finally able to start living again. Here's what Charlotte loves about her life now:

'I really appreciate being able to do the school runs because there was a long time when I couldn't do anything like that. I'd be

looking out the window, waving them off, seeing other people go off on the school run, and that was just my absolute dream – to do that with them. And I still love doing it now.

You know, I used to be a real worrier. I'd worry about ridiculous things. And then the worst thing that I hadn't even imagined happening happened to me – and you would think that would make my anxiety much worse. But in a way, it kind of freed me because it felt like the worst thing had happened. I'd never predicted it, and I couldn't have done anything to stop it, and when it did happen, as terrible as it was, I did find a way through it. I did manage to live my life day-to-day – and I did come out the other side. That's not to say, now that life has become much more normal again, I'm completely carefree. You start to find little anxieties creeping in over small things. But I can take a step back and think, "Remember what things were like and how desperate you would have been to be managing a tantrum about homework or feeling frustrated about them not getting ready in the mornings". And at the moment, sometimes, yes, it's still stressful, but I can take a step back and realise how lucky I am.'

And eventually, Charlotte felt well enough to relaunch her Colour Me Beautiful image consulting business.

'Something changed this year. I'm not sure what it was, but I suddenly felt like I would actually quite like to be doing something for me. Being a mum and a patient has defined me for such a long period of time. My mum is a Colour Me Beautiful consultant. She has a business, and she's done really well with it over the past few years. It gives her so much joy. She is young for her age because her job gives her such a boost; it energises her, and I felt like I needed a bit of that.

Initially, I was putting up obstacles – like I would have to build a website, work on my pricing, and all those things. But then, when it came to the idea of actually doing consultations, I thought – I can still do that. I felt I could return to that tomorrow, and I'd be fine. So I put the idea of how many jobs I'd have to do to one side and thought, what do I actually need to do to start? Well, I need to get my kit out and sort it out. I need to somehow put myself out there. I still had my Facebook page, which had been dead for the last several years, but I thought I could use that as a starting point because I've got a lot of old clients on there. I know newer friends will support me. So I got my kit out and then posted on my Facebook page that I was starting to see a few clients very slowly. I'd had a few friends express an interest, and suddenly, I had a few bookings. So I just started seeing a few friends, and then, a few weeks later, I thought I had created my own website before, I'm sure I could throw something up. So, in my spare time, I designed a website, and things took off from there. I've just really taken things one step at a time. But it's been lovely to get back to it. It's giving me another identity and another thing to focus on.'

Case Study – Nicola Lee, Sales Manager at Jewson

Nicola Lee, a sales manager at Jewson, was flying high in her career when she discovered a lump in her breast. Here's her experience of a cancer diagnosis and how that changed her perspective on life and work:[2]

'I found a lump in 2021. And because there was so much awareness around at that time, I knew the signs. I looked at it myself in the mirror and immediately knew it wasn't good. I went to

see my GP, who was amazing, and he referred me to a hospital right away. Two weeks later, they told me I had breast cancer. It was aggressive – stage 2. At the time, they didn't know what type of cancer it was. But it turned out it was hormonal cancer. I was lucky as I could have it cut out. They removed the lump and lymph nodes because it had started to spread. And then, from there, I had radiotherapy. Thankfully, I didn't need chemotherapy.

It's funny because in 2020, I'd had a bit of a bump in my career, where things weren't going quite so well, and I was mentally struggling with quite a lot at home. Jewson had been amazing and arranged for me to see a therapist. I only had six short sessions with this wonderful therapist who gave me cognitive behavioural therapy. But I think without having done that, I would have spiralled a lot quicker with the breast cancer diagnosis.

Getting a cancer diagnosis is a bit like grief. When you tell people you have cancer – it's like telling them that somebody has passed away. And you're suddenly managing everybody else through it, too. But a positive outlook definitely helps. You know, you can have really bad days and bad hours, and you can even have a really bad 15 minutes. But that's ok. Positive thinking is a great lever and strength. Knowing you are responsible for yourself and your own mindset is important.

I had my cancer during COVID, and I couldn't have visitors. I went to appointments and had the operation by myself. My husband would wait in the car park, and I'd come out and sometimes say – "That didn't go well." But he would say, "But you're getting help. You're being treated by people who know what they're doing. They know much more about breast cancer than we do. So let's go with what they're saying." And I liked that mindset to get us through it.

Even when I had my radiotherapy, I worked – I kept working. I had a few meltdowns about coming back to work. I had a nasty burn after my last radiotherapy session, which is normal, and I

had a bit of a panic attack about coming back. But I phoned my
direct manager and said, "I don't think I can return. I'm in a
lot of pain". And he just said, "Hey, it's fine. See how you feel on
Sunday. If you don't feel like it, text me. If you feel like it. I'll see
you on Monday". And it was just his kind of relaxed perspective
that took the pressure off.

I think what my cancer diagnosis has taught me is that you
have to use your experiences in life and learn from them. You have
to live the best life you can and do the things you enjoy. There will
be mundane things like organising the food shop, putting stuff in
the car, making sure there are dinners for everybody, and doing
the swimming drops. But I definitely think going through an expe-
rience like breast cancer gives you a brighter outlook on life.'

Nicola did return to work and is now a sales manager at Jewson with eight direct reports.

Case Study – Ali Fanshawe, Adoptive Mum of Two with Founder of FizzyKids

When Ali and her husband decided to adopt two children, like all new parents, they expected their lives to be turned upside down; however, they were thrown a curveball when both of their children were diagnosed with additional needs after starting primary school, including autism spectrum disorder (ASD), dyspraxia, and reactive attachment disorder. Here are some of the behaviours that Ali's children displayed that led to their diagnoses:[3]

'80% of children in a mainstream school classroom will operate
in pretty much the same way. They can sit on the carpet and
listen to their teacher. They'll be able to sit on a chair at the table
and complete a certain task. They'll be able to go out to play and
have 20 minutes of fun running around, maybe a bit of pushing

Staying Positive When Life Throws a Curveball

or shoving. But generally, they'll be okay. My children and lots of other children with additional needs or special needs will not operate in that way. If a teacher asks them a question, they might ignore them – it's almost like they haven't heard them. But really they might just not have had time to process the question. They might be unable to sit still at a table for a long time without distracting another child, or complete a simple task. They might struggle with reading, focus or attention. They might be outwardly more defensive or aggressive to other children, and they might use words or say things that sound a bit odd to adults, for example, using rude, inappropriate, or sexualised language in the wrong context at a young age – even if that language is not used at home.

A good school and teacher will usually pick up if something is not quite right. There are many routes to a diagnosis. I wish it were straightforward. It is not. Your GP is always a good place to start. They'll possibly refer you to CAMHS, the child and adult mental health service. You can also get a private diagnosis through psychologists and psychiatrists. Facebook groups are a brilliant way to identify local diagnosis support groups or professionals who can help you.'

Ali's eldest son's additional needs led to him moving from mainstream education to a specialist school. However, this does not always provide the solution a child requires, and after a challenging few years, he is now at home full time. Ali is now solely responsible for managing his funding package from the Local Authority and the education he receives at home and in the local community. As you can imagine, she has found it difficult to find a job that works around this. Following her experience raising two children with additional needs, Ali set up the brilliant website and podcast FizzyKids – a fantastic resource that provides support and advice for parents of children with additional needs.

'FizzyKids was about me learning to accept my children's needs and realising that I had to be a different kind of parent than the ones I was parented by! Standard parenting techniques were not giving me results. I wasn't getting anywhere with them, and it was causing chaos. It was only when I recognised this that I realised the way I had learnt to parent was not how I needed to parent my children. I went on an evolution – that's the only way I can describe it – of learning to parent differently, following therapeutic parenting techniques. The main difference between therapeutic parenting and more standard parenting is that you always do some therapeutic work in everything you say and do with your kids. They won't realise that you're doing it, but you do. The other thing about therapeutic parenting is that it's designed not just to help your children but, more importantly, to help you as the parent. One of the most critical things about helping parenting children with special needs, particularly those who have challenging behaviours, is that you stay regulated as a parent because you are the sole focus in their lives and possibly the only person at that point who will be able to help them stay regulated. And when I say regulated, I mean calm, not stressed.

Having therapeutically parented my children for quite a big chunk of their childhood, I'm often able to move back into some standard parenting – and it now works. It works because they trust me. They know I won't overreact because they don't see me as a threat. They don't think the world will end just because I've told them off.

I wanted to share my knowledge and journey with other parents who were going through the same thing – hence the birth of FizzyKids. At the moment, we offer several online courses for parents. There are also some free cheat sheets. Having had to leave my own job because of my kids with special needs, I wanted to help just one other parent get to the end of the day

51

without feeling utterly frazzled, exhausted, or ashamed. That was the mission behind FizzyKids.'

Ali has a final point for any employers out there, managing an employee who is also parenting or caring for a child with additional needs:

'Work can be a lifeline for parents of children with additional needs and provide them with an outlet if a lot is happening at home. Make sure you communicate regularly with your employees about what they need to feel supported and work effectively. Flexibility is key. If they're a parent of a special needs child, they might have a medical appointment, and if it's with the NHS, they just have to go. Being kind and understanding goes a long way.'

So, there you have it. Life doesn't always go according to plan, and sometimes, your career might need to take a back seat. Whether dealing with personal health issues, caring for family, or juggling the complexities of raising children with additional needs, these challenges don't spell the end of your professional journey. Instead, these hurdles often endow you with a richer set of skills, a deeper understanding of the human condition, and a renewed perspective on what truly matters. Remember, it's not about the obstacles themselves, but how you navigate them that defines your career trajectory. Keep pushing forward, pivot and adapt as needed, and let these experiences enrich, not hinder, your professional life.

Summary

Life Happens: Life throws curveballs, and sometimes work has to take a back seat. This chapter has been filled with stories from women who've faced serious challenges, like illness or caring for kids with special needs. They've shared how they managed to keep their careers going or even start new ventures inspired by their struggles to hopefully inspire you that when life gets in the way – anything is still possible!

You Can Turn Tough Times into Career Wins: Getting knocked down by life doesn't mean you've lost your professional skills, experience, or knowledge. The women featured here show that battling through personal tough times can actually make you better at your job. They've gained fresh perspectives and new skills that have made them more valuable in the workplace.

Find a Supportive Network: Getting through hard times means leaning on others. These stories highlight the importance of reaching out for help, using your network, and not being afraid to switch directions if it means keeping your career on track.

The Right Mindset is Key: Whether it's getting back into work after a break, kicking off a business inspired by personal experiences, or just finding a new path, the key ingredients are resilience and determination. These stories prove that it's possible to reinvent your career, no matter how large the obstacles.

Essentially, this chapter has shown that your career doesn't have to suffer even when life gets messy. With the right mindset, support, and some flexibility, you can overcome personal challenges and still achieve professional success. And it's true what they say – often, the detours we take in life provide the most interesting journeys!

Notes

1. Elizabeth Willetts (2023). Resilience Refined: Charlotte Ralph's Inspiring Journey Through Cancer, Motherhood, and Entrepreneurship. *Work It Like A Mum* (podcast) 23 November 2023. MP3 audio, 47:51, www.buzzsprout .com/2046830/14002544-resilience-refined-charlotte-ralph-s-inspiring-journey-through-cancer-motherhood-and-entrepreneurship. Accessed 1 August 2024.

2. Elizabeth Willetts (2024). Want to Thrive in Your Career After Kids? Here's How One Woman Crushed It (And Even a Cancer Diagnosis Hasn't Stopped Her). *Work It Like A Mum* (podcast) 21 March 2024. MP3 audio, 41:33, www.buzzsprout.com/2046830/14732476-want-to-thrive-in-your-career-after-kids-here-s-how-one-woman-crushed-it-and-even-a-cancer-diagnosis-hasn-t-stopped-her. Accessed 1 August 2024.

3. Elizabeth Willetts (2024). Redefining Success: Parenting Children with Additional Needs with Ali Fanshawe, *Work It Like A Mum* (podcast) 28 March 2024. MP3 audio, 48:32, www.buzzsprout.com/2046830/14757273-redefining-success-parenting-children-with-additional-needs-with-ali-fanshawe. Accessed 1 August 2024.

Gender Discrimination

Back in my recruitment agency days, I remember very clearly recruiting a qualified accountant for a small private equity firm in the Mayfair area. They actually had a pokey little office but were situated on one of the UK's most expensive streets. The company was steeped in history and run predominantly by old white men (the receptionist may have been the exception, if I recall). I was lucky – I had been given the job to fill exclusively (this means I didn't have any competition from other agencies). I helped the client screen CVs, arrange first interviews, shortlist for the final interview, etc. Anyhow – we got down to the last two candidates – both women – equally qualified and tough to choose between. One candidate was in her late 40s, and the other was about 30. I clearly remember the client calling me one Friday afternoon to tell me which candidate he wanted to offer the job to. It was the lady in her late 40s. He said without shame why they had decided to offer that candidate the job instead of the younger lady – because they were concerned that the younger woman might get pregnant and take maternity leave. To my shame, I didn't challenge this. In my defence, I was in my early 20s at the time and just happy to make a fee in a sales-driven environment.

But I knew then, as I still know now, that once women hit 30 and get married, society views them differently. And, whether she wants children or not, her biology can hold her back in the workplace.

So, gender bias in the workplace – this could be its own book. And yes, the Equality Act of 2010 is meant to protect those at work with certain protected characteristics, including age, disability, pregnancy and maternity, race, religion, or sex (amongst others), and the Equal Pay Act of 1970 prohibits paying women less for doing the same job as men; but unfortunately, gender bias and discrimination at work has not gone away.

And women often find themselves the victim of the motherhood penalty before becoming mothers! Don't believe me? Then how about this comment one of our Facebook group members received just after she got married – and no, she wasn't pregnant – *'I'm not bothering to ask you if you want to be on this project as you just got married, so will be off on maternity leave by this time next year...'.*

Or the 54,000 women who find themselves out of a job – or sidelined at work after announcing their pregnancy or during maternity leave whilst their (often less capable) male colleagues are leaping ahead.

Case Study – Donna Patterson, Founder of Let's Talk Work

Just before Donna Patterson found out she was pregnant, she was climbing the career ladder and about to go for a new role. Here was her experience:[1]

> *'I found out I was pregnant, and I had, just before that, been approached about a role in the business that I thought would be a bit of a challenge but something that I was up for giving a go. So then, as I said, I found out I was pregnant, and I thought for absolute transparency, I should disclose that information because, at the point at which I would be taking the role, based on my date, I would be due to go on maternity leave quite soon after. I didn't think it was fair not to lay my cards on the table. And as soon as I did that, the reaction was visible.*

What was said was – "Right – let's go and just look at the dates and see how that's going to work because I'm not quite sure if the dates will work now".

And that was it. There was no other formal follow-up. There was no other discussion about it. Admittedly, I didn't do any-thing about it, I didn't raise any flags to anyone. I did mention it to my line manager, who raised his eyebrows to sort of say that he didn't necessarily agree with what happened, but he didn't do anything about it either. And that was it. So, I was left in the role I had been in for quite a while, and nothing was said about this other role. As I said, I didn't flag or raise formal complaints. But the reason for that, I now understand, is that quite often, when you're pregnant or know you're going on maternity leave, you feel pretty vulnerable. You don't want to get a reputation as a trouble causer, and I now realise, in hindsight, that that didn't benefit me at all.'

Throughout her pregnancy and subsequent return to work, Donna faced workplace discrimination. Her attempts to resolve the issues were ignored or dismissed.

So yes, workplace discrimination and bias happen – if they didn't, we wouldn't have a gender pay gap, which happens when compa-nies have more men in more senior (higher-paying roles) and more women in more junior (lower-paying roles). At the time of writing, the gender pay gap in the UK stands at 14.3%. Globally, women won't receive pay parity with men until 2154. And in the UK, we have Equal Pay Day driven by the Fawcett Society.[2] This day is usually in late November and marks the day in the year when, based on the gender pay gap, women stop being paid compared to men. In 2023 this meant, on average, working women take home £574 less than men each month (£6888 p.a.).

So, we know there is gender bias in our workplaces and society that's somehow preventing women from reaching pay parity with men. There is a myriad of reasons for this, including:

- a lack of well-paid flexible jobs – women are more likely to be caregivers and therefore more likely to need flexible working but are often punished with lower-paid, lower-skilled part-time jobs that offer them this;

- girls aren't encouraged or don't choose to go into higher-paid jobs in finance and law – and are over-represented in lower-paid sectors (such as care!) that society needs the most but values the least;

- women are more likely to take career breaks when their children are small and then often struggle to re-enter the workplace at the level they left (although, with this book, you'll hopefully minimise the chance of that happening);

- plain old discrimination.

But the good news is that Donna didn't take the discrimination she was experiencing at work lying down. She spoke to the charity Pregnant then Screwed, who have a free helpline, got herself a mentor, and took her employer to a tribunal. She won a huge £60,000!

How Can You Protect Yourself Against Workplace Discrimination?

So, although companies and society need to do more to help us all (and particularly women), achieve their full potential at work and be valued for their contribution, there are some things that, as Donna did, you can do to help yourself.

1. First things first, don't feel you need to disclose your last salary when applying for jobs. I know it's difficult – especially

if you are a people-pleaser, and heck, I used to ask my candidates the 'what was your last salary' question too, but this question is not doing any of us any good. Why, you ask? Well, recruiters want to know your current or previous salary as they use this data to measure your level of experience, value, and expectations. They then consider this information when deciding which roles to put you forward for and what salary to offer at the hiring stage.

So, by asking about your salary history, female candidates who tend to be paid less than men (yes, the gender pay gap starts to creep in before women have had children – even in those sectors that are predominantly female, such as teaching) and candidates who have emigrated here from a country with an unfavourable exchange rate are automatically disadvantaged.

But ultimately, this question disadvantages us all. Employers could be tempted to offer their job vacancies to the 'cheapest candidate'. Real-time salaries and productivity have stalled in the UK since 2007. Is the question, 'What was your most recent salary?' preventing us all from getting a pay rise?

2. Ask for full interview feedback when attending job interviews. If you don't get the job, you want to know why – not only so you can improve for next time, but because if there was any hint of discrimination during the process, you could sue the organisation. If you're suspicious, you can submit a subject access request (SAR) to the company (more details about how to do this are on the Information Commissioner's website). The business is then legally obliged to release any data (including emails that mention you). This could be the best way of getting the evidence you need to prove your suspicions about discrimination.

3. The same applies if you are selected for redundancy. You want to know why and if any discrimination was involved. These SARs are your friend for getting the whole story.

4. Keep meticulous records of any forms of discrimination you experience/see in the workplace, including the dates. If you decide to take your employer to a tribunal, you will be required to present this information. And don't be afraid to submit a SAR as above to get that all-important evidence. Be aware of the time limit for submitting a discrimination claim to ACAS. At the time of writing the time limit is three months minus one day from the last time you were discriminated against to raise a claim, but please do check the most up-to-date requirements on the ACAS website. You should also be aware that new draft legislation, proposed to come into force in April 2025 will make it illegal for mothers to be dismissed during the first six months of their return to work.

5. Call it out if you hear a male colleague is earning more than you or another female colleague for doing the same role! Speak to HR and get them to address it – and ensure you receive back pay for any period you earned less!

And if you find yourself having been made redundant, there are some important steps you can take to ensure it was a fair and proper process:

1. Ask your ex-employer why you were made redundant – what the selection and assessment process was, and if you can be sent it.

2. Check whether you have the right to appeal against the redundancy, as this may give you some answers. Failing that, raise a grievance, which can be done in writing if you are already an ex-employee – this also helps if the case ends up in a tribunal.

3. Speak to an employment solicitor – many offer initial free consultations, and many home insurance policies cover legal costs, so it's worth checking your documents.

4. ACAS has a free helpline; its team offers brilliant advice. They can help you if you decide to pursue your case and will guide you through early conciliation (a process before the tribunal that hopefully will prevent your case from going that far if your ex-employer decides to settle). Remember, you have six months less one day to start your claim, so you have to be quick.

5. Document everything that has ever been said to you – you may need it as evidence.

6. Finally, don't forget to make that SAR. Your employer is legally required to release any data that refers to you, including emails, and it could provide the evidence you need to prove you've been discriminated against. Information can sometimes be missing or withheld; make sure you check the dates and correspondence chains.

Donna has now set up an organisation called Let's Talk Work, which is a destination for individuals who anticipate uncomfortable workplace conversations or anyone who is trying to negotiate a return to work but is worried about challenging conversations they may face.

Let's Talk Work can also provide knowledge and the practical support needed to help navigate the employment tribunal process if you decide to pursue a claim.

Here's Donna's final piece of advice for anyone feeling undermined at work:[3]

'Raise it. It doesn't need to be confrontational. It doesn't need to be difficult or hard. I admit it will be uncomfortable. But if you can't do it directly with the person, or if you can't do it through your line manager, find somebody else in your organisation, whether it's somebody in HR, employee relations, or another manager that you have worked with in the past, just find somebody that you trust in that business and say, "this has happened *to me', or I' have seen this happen to somebody else, and it's making me really uncomfortable and I want something to be done about it". And if you don't find that you're being listened to, then I think there's cause for concern there...*

By keeping quiet, not being a trouble-causer, keeping your head down', getting your work done, and being really grateful for that little tiny sliver of humanity that you get, you won't get the results you deserve. You don't get treated any better for not raising things up. In actual fact, I go so far as to say that by not raising the flag and bringing this to people's attention, you're allowing that behaviour to continue...

The reason why I set up Let's Talk work is for more people to build the confidence to take action against bad employers, forcing those employers to face the discriminatory behaviours and treatments that occur in their workplaces – and take action to prevent them from happening in the future.'

If you agree with Donna and want employers to stop discriminating against people at work, arm yourself with the facts about your rights, don't be afraid to make some noise and, as Donna has called her organisation – talk. The more people share their experiences, the more empowered we are collectively to stop bad workplace behaviour, setting a better standard for generations to come.

Summary

Recognise and Address Gender Bias: Learn to identify both overt and subtle forms of gender discrimination in your workplace. Understand that regardless of intention, these biases can significantly impact your career progression and sense of worth in your job.

Understand Your Rights: While laws like the Equality Act of 2010 and the Equal Pay Act of 1970 are designed to protect you, the reality often falls short. Discover how to leverage these laws effectively to challenge unfair practices and assert your rights.

Take Action Against Discrimination: Be inspired by stories of individuals like Donna Patterson, who successfully challenged discriminatory practices and won. These examples highlight the importance of standing up for your rights and the potential positive outcomes of doing so.

Empower Yourself with Practical Steps: Gain practical advice on advocating for yourself in the workplace, from negotiating salaries without revealing past compensation to using subject access requests to uncover discrimination. Learn the importance of documenting instances of bias and the steps to take if you need to challenge your employer legally.

Notes

1. Elizabeth Willetts (2024). How This Mother Took Her Employer to an Employment Tribunal – Without Legal Representation – And Won a Whopping £60,000 in Compensation. *Work It Like A Mum* (podcast) 9 March 2023. MP3 audio, 58:28, www.buzzsprout.com/2046830/12405823-how-this-mother-took-her-employer-to-an-employment-tribunal-without-legal-representation-and-won-a-whopping-60-000-in-compensation. Accessed 5 August 2024.
2. The Fawcett Society (2023), Equal Pay Day 2023 is November 22nd, hwww.fawcettsociety.org.uk/news/equal-pay-day-2023-is-november-22#:~:text=Jemima%20Olchawski%2C%20Chief%20Executive%20of,the%20end%20of%20the%20year. Accessed 5 August 2024.
3. Elizabeth Willetts (2024). How This Mother Took Her Employer to an Employment Tribunal – Without Legal Representation – And Won a Whopping £60,000 in Compensation. *Work It Like A Mum* (podcast) 9 March 2024. MP3 audio, 58:28, www.buzzsprout.com/2046830/12405823-how-this-mother-took-her-employer-to-an-employment-tribunal-without-legal-representation-and-won-a-whopping-60-000-in-compensation. Accessed 5 August 2024.

Chapter 7

Writing a CV

D id you know that recruiters spend on average just 10 seconds reviewing CVs, and a whopping 80% of CVs don't make it onto their shortlists? This chapter is dedicated to making sure yours isn't one of the 80%!

But perhaps you get brain freeze every time you go to write your CV. Maybe you're not sure where to start. Are you worried about how to fit everything into those all-important two pages? Or perhaps you don't feel like you have enough to say? Don't worry. By the end of this chapter, you'll know exactly how to structure your CV, what to write – and hopefully be itching to start.

So, without further ado, here's my step-by-step guide to quickly writing a brilliant CV that will help you land an interview for your dream job.

Step 1: CV Structure

Recruiters get hundreds of job applications per job advert. And to be blunt, they don't have time to spend hours reviewing your CV to see if you have the relevant skills and experience they're looking for. Therefore, you need to make an impact – fast! Start by making sure you've excluded all fluff. Your CV needs to be relevant and to the point. Think like a recruiter – what questions would they have regarding your application? The fewer question marks they have, the more likely you'll get to the top of their shortlist pile. Recruiters will initially skim your CV, so they will prefer your CV to follow a 'traditional' format so they know exactly where to find the information they are looking for. They want your CV to give them the information they're looking for easily and accessibly.

If you follow these simple steps when formatting your CV, you'll ensure it is clear and easy to read:

Appearance: Keep the font clean (Calibri or Arial) and easy to read (size 11 for the main points and 14 for the headings). Use black text on a white background. Don't include any fancy (i.e. distracting) graphics (unless you are applying for a graphic design job or similar). And please, no photographs. Unless you want to be the next Kate Moss, no one should (in theory) be interested in what you look like. It takes up valuable space on what should be a short document – and also runs the risk of creating a bias and opinion on you before you've even been met.

Personal Details: These should be at the top of your CV and include Name, Location, Email Address, Phone Number, and LinkedIn profile (if applicable). Please do not include your age, date of birth, marital status, or dog's name – you get my drift!

Personal Profile or Biography: This should be a few sentences directly under your personal details that tell the hiring manager who you are and your key experience. Think of it as a professional Instagram bio. If you're on a notice period of less than a week, include it here, plus your interview availability.

Career to Date: Start with your most recent job, then add previous jobs in reverse chronological order. Add your job title in a bold header, followed by your employer's name. Include dates employed 'from–until' (see my Top Tip below). If you've been in various roles with a single employer for several years, group them under a large heading, with each individual role under a sub-heading. This will help you avoid looking like a job hopper (if you haven't been) and also demonstrate that your previous employer valued you enough to promote you through several roles.

Here's an example:

Various roles due to promotion   November 2019–Present (see below)

Joe Blogs Company
    Office Manager   February 2022–Present

- Duty 1
- Duty 2
- Duty 3

    Team Administrator   November 2019–February 2002

- Duty 1
- Duty 2
- Duty 3

Now, similar to the example above, list your responsibilities under each job header using bullet points so they are easy to skim-read. Be specific about your role and duties, and avoid generalisations. 'Consider the Hiring Manager's perspective when writing about your responsibilities. You need to demonstrate your potential value to them, so ensure you include details about the impact you've previously made when completing each task. A good question to ask yourself when writing about previous roles is 'So what?' This will force you to expand on responsibilities and spell out the benefits you brought when doing your role - and therefore the value you can potentially bring elsewhere.'

Top Tip

If you have a career gap that you don't want to highlight or perhaps didn't stay with your previous employer for as long as you would have hoped, then put the dates employed to the right of the page. Placed here, they're naturally less visible (remember we read left to right). This keeps the reader focused on your job title, skills, and experience rather than how long you have worked somewhere (or been out of work for).

Education: Your education should go under work history – unless you are a school leaver or recent graduate. Start with your most recent education first and work backwards. Include dates attended, which institution, what you studied and grades (if you did well). You don't need to go as far back as GCSEs (unless you are applying for your first job). You should include A-Levels (or equivalent) and above. Add all relevant training and professional qualifications to this section.

IT Skills: Are you a whizz at Excel, have an excellent working knowledge of some fancy software package, or are you brilliant at designing PowerPoint presentations? Add this information to this section! Specific systems skills are often essential for certain roles, so don't forget to include all the bespoke (and more vanilla) systems you can use.

Languages: If you speak any languages, put them here, along with your fluency level. Being multi-lingual will make you stand out from the crowd and give you an edge over other candidates.

Full Driving Licence: Only add this if it is relevant to the jobs you are applying for (and applicable!).

References: DON'T PUT YOUR REFERENCE DETAILS ON A CV. If you put your actual referees on your CV, nothing stops the hiring manager from contacting them to find out more about you – even before inviting you to interview. This could put you in the awkward position of being forced to explain why you are looking for a new role if your referee is your current or most recent employer (and they should be at least one of your referees).

I'll also let you into a secret. Back in my recruitment agency days, if a candidate put referee details on their CV, a recruiter would be on the phone to these referees straight away. This would be in the hope of backfilling your vacancy (remember, this is before you have even secured an interview)! Your referee is now on a sales call that they'd rather not be on. If asked how the recruiter got their details, an inexperienced recruiter might let it slip that they came from your CV. You do not want to be in the bad books of someone who will do you a favour by (hopefully) providing a good reference. You provide references at the job offer and acceptance stage.

> **Top Tip**
>
> Considering the importance of formatting, I always advise sending CVs as a PDF rather than a Word document when applying for jobs. Although Word is best for editing, and therefore you should always work from a CV in Word, the format can change depending on which device it's viewed on, whereas PDF keeps its format – no matter what device. So, edit it in Word, but download it, and send it as a PDF, unless the recruiter asks otherwise.

Step 2: Use Relevant Keywords in Your CV

Right, cold, hard facts first – it's not always the recruiter or hiring manager who does the first CV sift. This task may be done by a computer (Applicant Tracking System) or an outsourced CV screener. This CV screener may be based abroad and not speak English as a first language. This individual (or computer) will do CV sifts for multiple jobs. They won't have spoken to the hiring manager and rely primarily on what is written in the job advert to decide whether you're suitable for the position. Therefore, your application will only pass the first sift if it contains the keywords and phrases asked for in the job advert. If they're not there, you will be rejected.

Therefore, make it easy for you (and the screener!). Fill your CV with the keywords used in the job advert. Don't be clever and use fancy alternatives or abbreviations. Pretend your mum is reviewing your CV against the job advert, and you can't go far wrong.

Step 3: What Impact Have You Made?

This is so important. What positive difference will be made to the organisation's bottom line (yes, even for back-office roles) by hiring you? Depending on the job vacancy, the hiring manager is funda-mentally interested in one of three things:

Can you save them time?

Can you save them money?

Will you make them money?

Maybe you are an accountant who previously automated a set of reports, saving hours at month end. Perhaps you work in procure-ment and negotiated a new contract with a stationery supplier, sav-ing thousands of pounds a year. You could be a salesperson who won a large contract with a prestigious client, bringing in significant revenue for your previous employer.

This is all great stuff that they want to know! Therefore, include some key achievements with quantifiable figures in each job section under their own sub-heading so they stand out.

When writing about your achievements, follow the STAR tech-nique (you can also use this when answering competency-based interview questions):

Situation: Share some context around the challenge faced.

Task: What was your responsibility in overcoming this challenge?

Action: What step-by-step action did you take to solve the problem?

Result: How did this benefit your employer? Did it save x amount of time, x amount of money, etc.?

Step 4: Look Professional

Your CV is a professional document that will (hopefully) be seen by your next boss. You want it to make the right first impression.

Therefore, if you have a silly email address from your teenage years, change it now! Use your first name dot surname at yahoo.com or hotmail.com (or similar) – something simple that won't create any negative preconceptions about you.

Top Tip

Consider what to call your document when you save it. For example, 'Elizabeth Willetts' looks cleaner and reads better than 'LizWilletts-01Feb2024'. It also makes your CV easier to find in a busy inbox.

Step 5: Keep it Short and Snappy

Your CV should be a mirror of the job advert. It just gives the hiring manager a flavour of who you are, what you have done, and your relevance to the role. Its main aim is to hook them in so they want to know more about you and invite you to interview. Therefore, they don't need to see the daily ins and outs of a role you did 10 years ago. Your last two jobs are the most important to focus on. You also don't need to include a complete list of every hobby you have.

Top Tip

If you are worried about going over two pages, reduce the margins to fit more words onto the page rather than reduce the font size, making your CV harder to read. If you really can't get your CV down to two pages because you have lots of RELEVANT experience, don't stress too much, but don't go over three pages.

Step 6: Check and Double-Check

I cannot tell you how important this is. Once you've finished writing your CV, please read it, read it, and then reread it. Then, send it to someone else to read through. A simple spelling mistake can cost you the interview – 'recruter', anyone?!? Poor spelling looks sloppy. It creates an impression that you will overlook things and make mistakes in the role.

Top Tip

Keep things consistent throughout your CV. If you use shortened months for dates employed for your first job, don't use longer ones for the next job.

To give you a head start with your CV, you can download a FREE CV template on my website at www.investinginwomen.co.uk/free-cv-template.

Crafting a CV that stands out in a sea of applicants can be daunting, but it's your first step towards landing that dream job. By following these simple steps, you will be well on your way to creating a CV that stands out for all the right reasons – and getting those all-important interview invitations.

Skills-Based CVs

Okay, let's talk about the elephant in the room, the rebellious cousin of the traditional CV: the skills-based CV. I'm not gonna lie; I'm not their biggest fan. The saying goes, 'A confused mind doesn't buy'. And this is exactly how I feel about a skills-based CV. Remember your CV is basically an advert for you, your skills and experience. I feel that skills-based CVs are a jumbled mess of keywords, lacking the clear timeline and narrative flow that I, as a busy recruiter starting my day with multiple applications to review, need to quickly assess if someone has the right skills and experience for the role I'm hiring for. And I know I'm not the only recruiter who feels this way. Yep – when I said we could receive hundreds of applications per role and therefore only have seconds to assess your CV, I wasn't lying.

To be honest, they feel like a candidate is trying to hide something, trying to distract you with glittery skills instead of solid experience. But I'm not here to judge; I'm here to inform. So, let's explore the world of skills-based CVs, shall we?

Why Use One?

Career Change: You're jumping ship, leaving the comfort of your current field for new pastures. A skills-based CV can showcase transferable skills, highlighting what you bring to the table when your job titles don't scream relevance.

Limited Experience: Fresh out of school or lacking years of formal experience? Skills-based CVs can put the spotlight on your skills and achievements, even if they come from volunteering, freelance gigs, or side hustles – although most recruiters understand fresh graduates' or school leavers' relative lack of experience and a traditional format should still serve you fine.

Gaps in Employment: Don't want to broadcast your career sabbatical or job hopping? This format can downplay the timeline, focusing on what you can do instead.

How to Do it Right (If You Must)

Tailor, Tailor, Tailor: Don't just copy and paste the same skills from job advert to job advert. Analyse each role, identify the key skills they need, and tailor your CV accordingly.

- **Quantify, Quantify, Quantify:** Numbers are your friend. Instead of just saying you're 'excellent' at communication, quantify your impact. Did you increase website traffic by 20% through your blog posts? Did your presentation save the company £5,000?

- **Use Strong Action Verbs:** Ditch the passive voice and let your skills shine. 'Managed a team of 10' becomes 'Led a team of 10 to achieve a 15% increase in productivity by...'

- **Keep it Short and Focused:** Remember, recruiters are busy. Aim for a maximum of two pages and prioritise skills relevant to the specific job.

- **Don't Ditch the Traditional Entirely:** Include a brief work history section, even if it's not the main focus. This gives context to your skills and proves you're not a complete mystery.

Final Verdict

Skills-based CVs aren't my cup of tea, but they can be a useful tool in specific situations. Just use them strategically, tailor them meticulously, and, for the love of all that is holy, avoid the keyword-stuffed mess. Remember, clarity and relevance are still king (or queen) of the CV world.

P.S. If you're still not convinced, feel free to stick to the tried-and-true traditional format. There's no shame in embracing your career history in all its glory and showcasing your experience in a clear, straightforward way. After all, a good CV is one that gets you the interview, regardless of its format.

Summary

- **Capture Attention Quickly:** Understand that recruiters spend an average of just 10 seconds reviewing CVs. Structure your

CV to highlight your most relevant experience and skills upfront, ensuring you make it onto the shortlist.

Structure is Key: Your CV should follow a traditional format to make it easy for recruiters to find the information they need. This includes a clean layout, personal details, a personal profile, a detailed career history, education and additional skills or languages.

Highlight Your Impact: Beyond listing your responsibilities, use the STAR technique to emphasise the tangible impact you've made in your roles. This helps recruiters see the value you could bring to their company.

Professional Presentation Matters: Ensure your CV is professionally presented, with a sensible email address and a filename that reflects your name professionally. Meticulously proofread to avoid spelling mistakes or inconsistencies.

Consider the Format: While traditional chronological CVs are preferred for clarity, skills-based CVs can be useful in certain situations, such as career changes or when emphasising transferable skills. However, they must be well tailored and clear to be effective.

Chapter 8

Cover Letters

Now, there are two schools of thought regarding cover letters. (1) 'They're not important, and no one reads them anyway' or (2) 'I reject anyone who doesn't send a cover letter'.

Personally, I sit somewhere in the middle. I don't think they're as important as your CV – and I certainly wouldn't reject the perfect candidate because they hadn't written a cover letter. But if you had two pretty much identical CVs – one had written a cover letter highlighting their relevant experience and expressing their interest in the role and company and the other had applied with just their CV and no cover letter to give any context – who do you think you would invite for an interview?

I think cover letters are particularly important if you're trying to switch careers and applying for a role completely different from your previous skills and experience. Cover letters help give context to this situation and prevent a hiring manager from scratching their head and thinking, 'Eh, why have they applied for this role?' With a cover letter explaining your reasons, they now understand, can see your transferable skills highlighted, and hopefully invite you for an interview.

They also come into their own when applying to smaller companies rather than larger corporations, where you might work directly with the founder. Team fit and enthusiasm can be more important than experience for some smaller firms. In this instance, a cover letter can also flatter the founder(s) and allow your personality to shine through.

But What Is a Cover Letter?

A cover letter is simply a letter or email addressed to the interviewer or hiring manager. It accompanies your CV when you apply for a job.

I think cover letters are an integral part of the application process. As I said – you can use them to highlight your key skills and strengths, emphasise your relevant experience, and demonstrate your enthusiasm for the role.

A cover letter is a great tool for sealing the deal, showing your personality, and encouraging a hiring manager to invite you for a job interview. Here are my top tips on how to create a great cover letter that will prevent you from blending in with all the other applications (and being honest – even just having one will help you stand out against the hundreds of other applicants who don't include one and give the impression they are spraying and praying with their applications).

Research

Before you start writing your cover letter, research the organisation. Who are they? What do they do? Who are their competitors? Have they been in the news recently – if so, why? The more you know about the organisation, the easier it will be to write about why you want to work there and why you are a good fit.

Who Should Your Cover Letter Address?

Ideally, you should personalise and address your cover letter to the person reviewing CVs. This information should be in the job advert. If not, try to track down the recruiter's or hiring manager's name on LinkedIn or the company website. You could always call the organisation and ask if you can't find the details.

Using the correct person's name will demonstrate your enthusiasm for the position and your initiative in obtaining their details.

If you still can't find their name, 'Dear Sir/Madam' will suffice.

How Should You Structure Your Cover Letter?

Following your greeting, the first paragraph should set the context for the letter and highlight why you are getting in touch.

For example: *'I would like to apply for the Financial Accountant position that I saw advertised on the Investing in Women job board. I have enclosed my CV for your consideration.'*

The second paragraph should talk about your suitability for the vacancy. Refer to the job advert to see what the expected duties are and the keywords used. Draw out any relevant experience and pepper this paragraph with these exact keywords (if applicable). This will help ensure your application gets through any automated applicant tracking system used to pick out keywords and decide which candidates to shortlist.

For example: *'As you will see from my CV, I am an ACA Qualified Accountant with four years of PQE. I have experience preparing accounts within large organisations, producing advanced financial modelling, meeting tight deadlines, and working with various stakeholders.'*

The third paragraph should include details of why the organisation should hire you and highlight your key achievements related to the skills needed for the role.

For example: *'In my current role, I have streamlined and automated various processes using financial modelling and advanced Excel, resulting in a time saving of 2 days at month's end.'* (Remember, recruiters like to see measurable achievements.) To help you write this paragraph, refer to the STAR technique discussed in Chapter 7 on CVs. You can also write about your achievements in bullet points, making them stand out on the page.

In the fourth paragraph, you should reiterate your enthusiasm for the vacancy, using the job advert as a guide, weaving in your research on the organisation.

For example: *'I believe I will be a great hire for your organisation and bring the same level of dedication, innovation and enthusiasm that I have brought to previous roles. With your recent success with X and my experience in advanced automation and financial modelling, I am confident we will be a great fit. I will be able to quickly add value and contribute to your continued growth and success.'*

End on a High

Do not feel you can only apply for a role if you meet all the job requirements. Some studies show that women only apply for a job if they meet 100% of the requirements, whilst men will apply if they meet 60%.

A role should stretch you, there's an argument that if you can do everything required from day 1, you're not progressing in your career and will quickly become bored in the role.

But don't use a cover letter to apologise for any experience you don't yet have. Instead, reiterate your interest in the position and add a call to action.

For example: *'Thank you, PERSON NAME, for taking the time to review my application. As you will see from my CV, I am a strong candidate for the role with the relevant skills and experience you are looking for. I look forward to meeting you to discuss my application further.'*

If you discover the person's name, sign off 'Yours Sincerely'. If your cover letter is addressed 'Dear Sir/Madam', sign off 'Yours Faithfully' followed by your name.

Keep it Short and Concise

As a rule of thumb, keep your cover letter to about half a page of A4. Any longer, and you risk boring the reader. Any shorter, and you won't have covered all the points in enough depth.

Don't Forget

Once finished, proofread your cover letter to check for any spelling mistakes. Poor spelling looks sloppy and gives the impression you will overlook areas of your role. Use this opportunity to edit out any unnecessary words or phrases.

As a general rule, don't mention salary expectations just yet unless the organisation has explicitly asked for that information.

To be consistent, use the same font as in your CV. Avoid using fancy (i.e. distracting) graphics and pictures.

Remember to tailor your cover letter to each job advert rather than sending a generic cover letter for each role. When you take the time to tailor your cover letter (and CV) for each position, you have the opportunity to sell yourself, your skills, and your experience to the hiring manager, and your application will stand out against the other applicants.

Double-check the employer and hiring manager's names. The easiest way to guarantee NOT to be invited to an interview is to address your cover letter to the wrong person.

And finally – be confident when writing your cover letter that you are the perfect applicant for the job. The fact that you are reading this book now shows that you are a conscientious and diligent individual. Your next employer will be lucky to have you.

Crafting a cover letter that captures your essence and professional prowess is an art. If you truly want to make your application shine, a great cover letter should speak volumes about your unique value and resonate with the recruiter. Follow the steps above, and you'll be well on your way...

Remember to check out the cover letter template at the end of this book. It will help you structure your cover letters so you include all the information an employer is looking for and sell your experience and value to them.

Summary

A Cover Letter is Important: While not as crucial as your CV, a well-crafted cover letter can distinguish you from equally qualified candidates, especially in career transitions. It provides context for your application and highlights your enthusiasm for the role.

Personalisation is Key: Research the company and address your cover letter to a specific person. Personalising your letter shows initiative and a genuine interest in the position.

Content Structure: Begin with an introduction to your application, followed by paragraphs that showcase your suitability for the role, relevant achievements, and enthusiasm for the company. Use keywords from the job advert to align your experience with what the employer seeks.

Conciseness and Confidence: Keep your cover letter concise, about half a page of A4, focusing on your strengths and how you can contribute to the company. End with a confident call to action, inviting the hiring manager to discuss your application further.

If you're a job seeker, you need to be on LinkedIn. With over 1 billion users, it's the largest professional social networking platform globally and THE social media network of choice for recruiters and employers. So, if you're afraid about going onto LinkedIn because you're worried it's too corporate or your old boss might see you, it's time to get over yourself because you're missing out on a goldmine of potential opportunities. The amount of people who get head-hunted for their dream job through LinkedIn is astronomical. And even though there are over 1 billion users on the platform – many of them business decision-makers and leaders – only 1% of members actually post content, so unlike the highly saturated and competitive Instagram and TikTok, there's a great opportunity for you to build a personal brand on LinkedIn too – great if you want to become one of the most highly sought after individuals in your industry, a wannabee thought leader, or would like to build your own business.

But back to job hunting and using LinkedIn as your partner in crime to help you get found for your dream job.

Like all good things, LinkedIn starts with the basics – the most basic being your LinkedIn profile.

So, What is a LinkedIn Profile?

According to LinkedIn: 'Your LinkedIn profile is a professional landing page for you to manage your own, personal brand. It's a great way to tell people who you are and what you do by displaying a general history of your professional experiences and achievements.'[1]

You can use your LinkedIn profile to add a more personal and informal touch than your CV might show. Remember, your LinkedIn profile should complement rather than replace your CV and show who you are and a bit of your personality in a way a CV can't.

Why Is a LinkedIn Profile Important?

Apart from being the world's largest professional social media platform, LinkedIn is also a leading job board and the social network that recruiters and employers use to find potential candidates to fill their job vacancies. Even just having a presence on there is an excellent way to be approached about your ideal job vacancy rather than constantly applying for new roles.

Therefore, if you're looking for a new job, you can't afford not to be on LinkedIn. Through the platform, your dream role can (literally) fall into your lap (or LinkedIn inbox, to be precise).

Right – Let's Start From the Beginning

So, we've established why you need to be on LinkedIn. Now, let's talk about how to write this puppy so you stand out to your dream employer against the other 1 billion people already on there.

1. Choose a good profile picture. It doesn't need to have been taken by a professional photographer, but this is not Instagram. You should choose one where you look smart and professional and are smiling directly at the camera. Don't use a photograph of you from a night out. It should be a photo of just you – not you with your mates. If you don't have a good picture, ask a friend to take one and use that. Photos humanise your profile and are one of the first impressions a recruiter

will have of you. You can also add a banner image at the top of your profile with more details about who you are and what you do. You can download some professional-looking customisable templates from Canva that you can change to suit your test and the image you want to portray.

2. Change the custom URL field. When you create your LinkedIn profile, the URL will look like this:

linkedin.com/pub/yourname/29/890/2b9/

But you can easily change it to look like this:

linkedin.com/in/your-name

Not only does this look more professional and show you have an eye for detail, but it also makes you easier to find on LinkedIn.

So – how do you change your URL?

a. On your profile, click on the text that says contact info. This will then take you to your public profile settings. In the top right-hand corner, click to edit your custom URL, and choose your first and last name if possible.

b. While here, also ensure you've not accidentally set your profile to private. You don't want to spend all this time and effort creating a flippin' amazing LinkedIn profile and then not have anyone be able to find you.

3. Make sure you've switched on public visibility outside of LinkedIn; others can see your full name and headline, profile edits are switched on so your network is notified of your job changes and any new certificates you obtain, and all settings are made public.

Great – we haven't accidentally hidden ourselves from view.

PROFILE VISIBILITY - MAKE SURE YOU GET FOUND

Click settings - find them by clicking the little arrow under your profile photo on your homepage

← Back

Off-LinkedIn Visibility
Show information from your profile to users of permitted services such as Outlook?
Learn more

Profile visibility outside LinkedIn   On 🔘

You can also manage whether your profile information can be found using your email address or phone number.

Through our partnerships and developer program, we enable certain affiliates, partners, customers, and other permitted developers to display to their users, information from the profiles of members. Changing the above setting doesn't limit visibility on search engines, which is controlled by the public profile setting.

Ensure profile visibility outside of LinkedIn is on.

PROFILE VISIBILITY

Clicking here will also show you more advanced profile public visibility settings - make sure all these are on and your profile picture can be found by public

PROFILE VISIBILITY

Click edit public profile & URL - linkedin.com/pub/yourname/2 9/890/2b9/

Public profile settings

You control your profile and can limit what is shown on search engines and other off-LinkedIn services. Viewers who aren't signed in to LinkedIn will see all or some portions of the profile view displayed below.

Flexible Jobs - Free CV Template - Career Advice - Podcast - Community

Investing in Women

Sign up for my newsletter & get a free CV template, career inspiration, exclusive invites and the latest jobs straight to your inbox

Sign up!

🔗 **Edit your custom URL.**

Personalize the URL for your profile.

www.linkedin.com/in/elizabeth-willetts ✏

🖊 **Edit Content**

This is your public profile. To edit its sections, update your profile.

Edit contents

👁 **Edit Visibility**

You control your profile's appearance for people who are not signed in to LinkedIn. The limits you set here affect how your

By clicking on public profile and URL you can easily change it to look like this:

linkedin.com/in/your-name

Not only does this look more professional and show you have an eye for detail, but it also makes you easier to find on LinkedIn.

PROFILE VISIBILITY

Make sure profile edits are turned on - so your network gets informed about on all your fantastic achievements

← Back

Sharing profile edits

Should we notify your network of key profile changes (such as new job, education, certificate, profile video) and work anniversaries?

Share key profile updates   On 🔵

Learn more about sharing profile updates.

PROFILE VISIBILITY

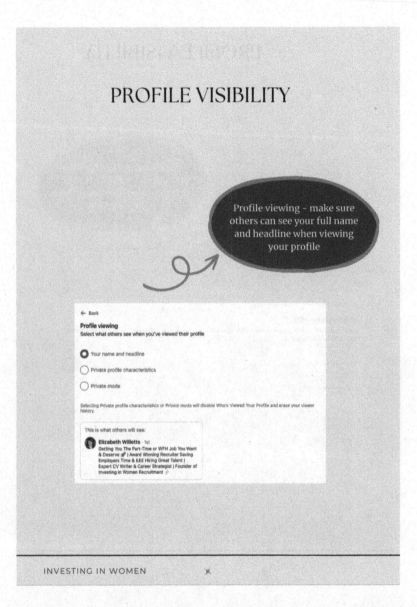

Profile viewing - make sure others can see your full name and headline when viewing your profile

← Back

Profile viewing
Select what others see when you've viewed their profile

○ Your name and headline

○ Private profile characteristics

○ Private mode

Selecting Private profile characteristics or Private mode will disable Who's Viewed Your Profile and erase your viewer history.

This is what others will see:

Elizabeth Willetts · 1st
Getting You The Part-Time or WFH Job You Want & Deserve 🚀 | Award Winning Recruiter Saving Employers Time & £££ Hiring Great Talent | Expert CV Writer & Career Strategist | Founder of Investing in Women Recruitment 🚀

4. Write a standout headline. Your headline is the professional bio just under your name. Most people just write their job title. This is fine, but they are missing a trick by not utilising the opportunity this space gives them. Your headline and profile picture is also the only information shown when you appear in a recruiter's search or comment on someone's post. Therefore, it's a golden opportunity to attract your dream employer.

Include your target or existing job title key skills and strengths in your headline and highlight why you are a valuable employee. The key to a great LinkedIn profile is to compel the reader to keep scrolling down the page – and a headline is what encourages them to click on your profile in the first place.

Your headline is also your first opportunity to hook the reader and encourage them to click on your profile and keep reading. Speak directly to your dream employer; be specific, concise and creative. And don't forget to use keywords to optimise your chances of being found in those searches.

5. Moving onto keywords, recruiters and employers use LinkedIn to search for potential candidates using keywords. Therefore, for the right people to find your profile – that is, those recruiting for your dream job – you need to ensure your profile is full of relevant keywords.

Look at some job adverts for roles you're interested in to decide which keywords to use. What words are used the most frequently? Now, put these exact words and phrases into your profile, and avoid using jargon or internal language.

6. We've now reached your 'about' section. This is a great chance to further summarise your key skills and experience in greater depth.

a. Who are you? What makes you tick? What have been your key achievements to date – use the STAR technique to help you write about these. I referred to these in Chapter 7, 'Writing a CV', but if you need a refresher, the STAR technique requires you to refer to a challenging Situation, elaborate on the Task you undertook to overcome the challenge, what you Achieved and the Result. Remember, we want to hear what *you* did – not the team, where it's unclear what your actual involvement was.

   b. What do you enjoy doing outside of work (remember, people want to work with people – and including interests is a great way to establish some common ground with others), and what are your career aspirations?

   Write this section using the first person – remember you're a person who wants to connect with another human being, and using third person sounds ever so corporate, stuffy – and being honest, poncey – on what is becoming a more friendly and community-based social media platform.

   c. If you're openly looking for work, you can end this section with a call to action, such as 'Send me a DM (direct message) if you want to learn more about my experience and how I can help your business thrive'.

7. Use your featured section to highlight any articles you have written, webinars or professional videos you have created, popular posts, etc. Again – this is a great way to help you stand out in a crowded job-seeking market.

8. Now, it's time to add your experience, just as you would on a CV. Include your employer's name, job title, and dates worked. Underneath each role, highlight your key skills and strengths. The aim here is to highlight your accomplishments and responsibilities engagingly, demonstrating what you did, how well you did it and what effect it had. Don't forget the keywords!

   You also add your education details and any additional training you might have done to the end of this section.

9. The finishing touches – to give your profile the extra wow factor, ask some current and ex-colleagues and clients for recommendations. Adding relevant recommendations to your profile

shows potential employers that other professionals are willing to vouch for you in a public forum. They get a reference before they even meet you, making a massive difference in the success of your job search.

a. You can also add and ask others to endorse you for your skills and industry knowledge – again, this makes your profile more searchable and improves your likelihood of being found by the right people.

b. Finally – if you are openly seeking work, don't forget to add the 'open to work' green banner that wraps around your profile picture. This banner tells potential employers you are actively looking for work and increases your chances of being approached for new roles.

Using LinkedIn for Networking

Now that we've created a profile that speaks to our ideal employer, we need to start connecting with them and building that all-important network. Refer back to the list you created in Chapter 1, 'What Do You Want?' There, you made a list of your dream employers. Now, start connecting with them! LinkedIn wants us to make connections, so type job titles of prospective hiring managers for your field and company names into the search bar and send a connection request. You can send a short note alongside your connection request. Something like: *I'm looking to build my network in the (your area) space (or 'at your company' if connecting with the recruiter), and I'd love to connect'.*

And that's it – nothing too ick, but it does the job and builds your network.

Don't forget to connect with the recruiters and talent acquisition managers at your ideal companies, too. It's also worth connecting with potential team mates at the companies you want to work for.

Once connected, you can find out more about their organisation/team so you know for sure if that team is the right one for you. You can also ask them about the types of candidates they like to hire so you can tailor your CV and LinkedIn profile to highlight your relevant skills and experience – and practice for the interview questions you'll likely be asked. Many large companies also offer referral schemes, whereby they pay their staff a bonus for referring someone to their role (it's a lot cheaper to do that than pay an agency fee). Therefore, these individuals may be more likely to refer you and put in a good word to their hiring manager if they know there is a reward at the end of it.

Don't send more than 10 connection requests per day when you first start sending them. If you send more than that, LinkedIn might view you as a spam or bot user and put you in 'LinkedIn Jail' – a place we want to avoid.

Once you've spent a couple of months sending 10 connection requests per day, LinkedIn will view you as a reliable and credible user, and you can increase the number of connection requests you send, building up to a maximum of 25 per day.

Now you've started building a valuable network, you want them to notice you. The easiest (and least daunting) way to be noticed and appreciated by your new connections is to simply comment on their posts and content. And commenting on others' posts and content is one of the fastest ways to build authentic relationships in an online world. By commenting on other people's content, you will become more comfortable being on LinkedIn (and I recommend you don't spend any more than 30 minutes a day there because, as we all know, social media is a time suck) and start to build up your confidence to create your own posts and content.

Posting on social media can be addictive. You have to be consistent to get long-term results and make the impact you want, but remember, only 1% of LinkedIn users create content, making it a great platform for you to build visibility. The more you post, the more visible you will become to your network of dream employers and valuable connections – and the more they will get to 'know, like, and trust you'. – helping you become more memorable to them. That's great news when they're next looking to hire and wondering if they know of any good potential candidates...

And once you're in the 1% of LinkedIn members regularly creating content, that's when you'll really see doors fly open that you thought were closed to you and opportunities land in your inbox that you'd never envisioned in your wildest dreams...

Posts can be a mixture of personal, work and news. And yes, while LinkedIn isn't Facebook, it has become more personal over the past five years. People want to work with people, so you can post about you – what you did at the weekend, your holiday, year in review, favourite book, why you started doing what you do, your thoughts on the latest industry trends, any networking events you've attended, what you wish you'd known when you were starting out, job tips and tricks, etc. Remember – you are interesting and will always be one step ahead (and therefore a role model) to at least one other person. I've added a month's posting plan to get you started at the end of the book, so writer's block is not an excuse for not posting.

LinkedIn is not a hypervisual platform like Instagram, but an image or video accompanying your post does help 'stop the scroll' and make it stand out – and photos of you are best so you become more familiar to your network. Make sure your posts aren't too text-heavy – no one has the attention span to read through masses of words on a social media platform. Think lots of white space, bullet points and emojis to make it visually appealing and easy to read – basically skimmable. End your post with a question to encourage engagement on your post – something the LinkedIn algorithm loves. You can also use a few relevant hashtags (five maximum).

And I'm begging you – don't post and ghost. If people do start to engage and comment on your post, make sure you reply and engage back – this will extend the reach of your post. Another trick for improving post engagement is commenting on other people's posts just before and after posting your content.

Experiment with different post styles – memes, images, photos, audio – and once you start getting really brave – video. Video is the quickest way to build 'know, like and trust' with your network and stand out on the platform. And yep, I know it's not for everyone; that's why I've put it last because I want you to enjoy being on LinkedIn, and if the thought of video makes you feel sick, then don't do it. But if you are confident being on camera, go for it! There aren't many people doing videos, so it is the quickest way to stand out and be seen as a thought leader in your industry.

Case Study

Leigh Welsh is one of the UK's leading personal branding strategists. He has spent over a decade building his own personal brand, with thousands of followers on LinkedIn and a female leadership community he's grown with his podcast, *She's a Leader*. He's the founder of Vidible, a personal branding and video marketing business which encourages individuals to think about their personal brand as much as they do their company brand. He's the mastermind behind the personal brands of some of the UK's most exciting entrepreneurs. But what is a personal brand, and should you create one?

Here's Leigh's take:[2]

> *'Personal branding is how people feel when they interact with you online. In our day-to-day lives, we naturally exude a personal brand. It may be at a networking event or when picking up your kids from school. Whatever you're doing on a daily basis, you're projecting an image. It's how others perceive you, how they warm to you, what they think about you and how they feel when they see you. That's what we're trying to get to in an online presence, specifically on LinkedIn. People think personal brand*

is reputation. But everyone has a reputation. It might be good, it might be bad, it might be indifferent. But we all have one based on our interactions with people and organisations.

On the other hand, personal brand is how YOU WANT people to see you. And you can promote that as much as you want. Personal branding is a conscious effort to portray who you really are. Sometimes, it's given a bad rep, and people associate personal brands with Instagram, Lamborghinis, and yachts – that kind of ego-driven personal branding – or they perceive a brand as only applicable to companies like Coca-Cola or Nike. But personal branding is somewhere in between. A personal brand creates a feeling that someone has when they interact with you or your content.

On a personal level, building a personal brand has not only elevated my career, but also my clients. When I work with people, I want their potential customers and clients to feel like they already know them. Because isn't that exactly where you want your business to be? What do the best and biggest brands in the world do? They create an emotion. You have a connection with that brand. You wear that brand because it provides you with a feeling. You follow the person behind a personal brand because they create a connection.

You don't want to build a personal brand just for likes on Instagram or to show off to your friends. It's for your current or potential employer to recognise your contribution and value. That is the biggest benefit. We're in an age now where it's not what you know; it's not even who you know – now it's who knows you!

Consider this: Any potential employer is going to look at you and your CV before that interview happens. But before that interview happens, they're also going to look at your social media – they'll be looking at your LinkedIn – and possibly your Facebook and Instagram. Are your social profiles emulating your personal

97

values? Are they demonstrating the value and expertise you can bring to an organisation? Are they selling you before you've even interviewed?

And if you're currently employed and have built a personal brand, it can add an extra layer of job security. Your employer has to consider not just the skill gap they'll lose if they lose you but also the impact on their company and employer brand. If you leave, what message does that send out to who may be your employer's potential or current customers? What will THEY think if you're made redundant?

Plus, if you're made redundant or want to look for a new role, a strong personal brand makes you much more desirable to potential employers – you're not just bringing yourself and your skill set – you can also bring a network of potential clients and be seen as a thought leader in your space.'

And if Leigh has convinced you of the benefits of building a personal brand but you're wondering how to start, here are his tips:

'The first step to building a personal brand is to identify your values [which you'll have done in Chapter 1]. *Remember, you're not try-ing to appeal to everyone – you want your content to resonate with employers and connections who share your values.*

And forget about creating. Start documenting. Document the journey you've been on, where you're trying to get to, the challenges you've had along the way, your failures, what you're passionate about, and why people might be interested. Every-body has a different story. And you and your stories are com-pletely unique. No one has been on the same journey. Giving people a glimpse of who you are, your life and your journey builds that connection.

Be as authentic as possible – don't think, "How will I position this post for that audience?" or "How shall I put this to resonate

Flex

with that demographic?" Just be authentically you! Don't try to be someone you're not. Get out there and start posting. Some people love writing and are really good at that, but they try to do videos because they think videos get more reach. But when you start, stick to what you feel comfortable with and know you're good at. Trying to make videos when you feel uncomfortable on camera will come through in the content you create and post. But remember, everyone improves over time. The only way you're going to improve is to get started. And don't worry about what other people think – people are much more supportive than you think. The more you do it, the better you'll get, and you will build that legion of adoring fans – NOT followers – who will vouch for you when you really need them.'

Some final tips – only a very small percentage of your followers will see your posts, so don't worry that you are 'repeating yourself', you are 'overexposed', 'showing off', etc. Most people are supportive of seeing others do well. If you can post two to three times a week, you'll get good exposure on the site to achieve your goals.

Keep your sentences and paragraphs short, with lots of white space in the text. People have short attention spans and tend to scroll. They won't stop to read your posts if they are hard to read and just a big block of text. Posts with pictures of you get more engagement and help build up the 'know, like and trust' with your audience – essential when building those relationships and establishing your credibility on the platform.

LinkedIn is a professional platform, but people buy from people and want to work with people – not corporate robots. So make it fun and let people get to know the real you and your interests – favourite TV programmes, books, what you did at the weekend. If you're uncomfortable sharing too much of yourself, you don't need to go overboard. Keep it light – imagine you were chatting with someone at a face-to-face networking event and trying to establish some common ground. A good rule of thumb is 2/3 business to 1/3 personal or 3/4 business to 1/4 personal, depending on what you are up to.

Summary

Why LinkedIn? LinkedIn has over 1 billion users and is a crucial social media platform for professional networking and job opportunities. Unlike other social media platforms, only 1% of LinkedIn users post content, offering you a unique chance to stand out by actively engaging, posting and sharing your insights.

Optimise Your Profile: Start with a professional photo and a custom URL to make your profile more accessible and appealing to potential connections, hiring managers and recruiters. Your headline and about section should succinctly highlight your skills, experience, and what makes you unique, using keywords relevant to your industry to improve your odds of being found in recruiters' searches.

Highlight Your Achievements: Utilise the featured section to showcase your professional accomplishments, articles, and projects. This not only enhances your profile but also provides tangible examples of your expertise and interests.

Build and Engage Your Network: Connect with industry leaders, potential employers, and colleagues and interact with their content. This increases your visibility and demonstrates your active involvement in your professional community. Sharing your own experiences, insights, and achievements helps establish you as a thought leader in your industry and build your personal brand, attracting some amazing opportunities directly to your inbox. An example of an opportunity that fell into my inbox is this book and a book deal that was offered off the back of my personal brand and network, which I'd spent years building – an editor at Wiley heard me being interviewed on one of my LinkedIn connection's podcasts. So you really don't know where your personal brand, LinkedIn profile and network will take you – and it all starts with just one post and taking the time to make those valuable connections…

So there you have it – a whistle-stop tour of LinkedIn profiles, networking, posting, building a personal brand and the mysterious algorithm. Like I said – forget TikTok – if you're looking for a new role, LinkedIn is where it's at. See you there!

Notes

1. www.linkedin.com/help/linkedin/answer/a564064/your-linkedin-profile?lang=en#:~:text=Your%20LinkedIn%20profile%20is%20a%20professional%20landing%20page,general%20history%20of%20your%20professional%20experiences%20and%20achievements. Accessed 5 August 2024.
2. Elizabeth Willetts (2024). How to Build a Career-Changing Personal Brand That Opens Doors With Leigh Welsh, *Work It Like A Mum* (podcast) 14 March 2024. MP3 audio, 44:12, www.buzzsprout.com/2046830/14678938-how-to-build-a-career-changing-personal-brand-that-opens-doors-with-leigh-welsh. Accessed 5 August 2024.

Chapter 10

Offline Networking

As someone who gets as nervous as the next person walking into a room full of strangers, I can sympathise with those who find networking daunting, but we all have a network – whether large or small. Your immediate network is your friends or family. Ask yourself – do they know what you do? We sometimes forget to tell those closest to us what we do and when we're looking for new opportunities, but your friends and family will be your biggest cheerleaders and advocates so tell them your plans!

Networking opportunities don't have to be formal affairs – at the local running club you might tell your running partner your career aspirations on your next jog, a friend on the school run that you're looking for a job-share partner, your auntie that you've launched a business and looking for new clients, or that you're looking for a secondment during the more informal networking meet-ups many large corporates host.

But all networking has something in common – it needs you to put yourself out there, be authentic and friendly, give and receive – and, most importantly, tell people what you do, the skills you have, and what you want.

Some of the most exciting things to have happened in my career have come through my network, including a book deal with Wiley to write the book you are holding now! But like all good networkers, I gave first. I invited personal finance expert Sammie Ellard-King to be a guest on my LinkedIn Live. He reciprocated the offer by inviting me to be a guest on his podcast, which was by chance listened to by an editor at Wiley, who asked to meet me and subsequently offered me a book deal!

And now, much of my business comes from building relationships and those all-important referrals.

In this chapter, I share the advice I've received from some amazing women (all of whom I've met through networking) that have built their careers and, in some cases, businesses by overcoming their fears and mastering the art of networking.

How to Make Networking Work for You

When Rebecca Newenham founded her outsourcing business, Get Ahead, 14 years ago, the thought of cold calling to win business did not appeal, but she knew she had to get herself 'out there' to make those all-important sales. So, Rebecca turned to local networking meetings to meet local business owners who might be interested in what Get Ahead had to offer. Although Rebecca was nervous attending her first few networking events, she has become such a pro that she now runs a regular LinkedIn Local networking event in her home town of Guildford, Surrey.

Here's Rebecca's experience of networking to grow her business:[1]

'I remember when I launched Get Ahead 14 years ago, I was panicking about the thought of making sales when someone said, "You've got to go to networking meetings; you've got to get out there." It immediately sent me back to that horror of some of my corporate jobs, where I was planted into a meeting and had no idea what I was talking about. And I think that's the big difference. Generally, networking, when it's authentic and means something to you, is so much easier because you're representing yourself and talking about things you're an expert in.'

There are different types of networking meetings, but Rebecca advises finding the one that's right for you. Here's what Rebecca has to say:

'It's finding what's right for you at the stage you're at – whether you're growing your business or looking for that next corporate promotion. Sourcing the most appropriate networking helps when you start thinking, "Where am I going to find the people I want to connect with? Where are they hanging out?" – and then finding them! The events can be structured – or not, but it's about you showing up authentically and feeling comfortable. And, if you feel daunted attending big events, you can carve out your own little comfort blanket within a larger group. So before going to an event, clarify what you want to achieve. It could be that I want to have three really good conversations with people, or I just want to relax and see where it goes. It's permitting yourself to set your own agenda before you even go to an event.

It can be helpful to get a hold of the attendee list beforehand so you can do a little bit of research about who's going to be there. Link in with them ahead of time so there's a friendly face when you walk into the room. And don't forget – when you're in a group and see someone coming, open out and allow people to come into your conversation because that's ultimately what you're there for – to meet and connect with people.'

Rebecca's final bit of advice to become a pro at networking is:

'Be the person you would like to meet! Be the person who's engaged, who's asking questions and is interested in the person you're talking to and listening to their answers. It's being a little bit brave, putting on your big girl pants and thinking, "Well, I'm here – I must make the most of it."'

Your Step-by-Step Guide to Becoming a Networking Pro

Someone who is definitely making the most of it – and all life has to offer – is Leanne Cooper, a career advancement coach who helps corporate female leaders accelerate their careers by transforming self-doubt into self-confidence so they can stop getting overlooked and start getting noticed.

Leanne's on a mission to make career confidence accessible for all women, so they recognise their strengths, realise their ambitions, and stand tall in careers together. She has the following advice for women nervous about attending networking meetings:[2]

- Spend time preparing

  - Support yourself in the run-up to these events. What you do before a networking event can really serve you well. Start the preparation phase by focusing on your relationship with yourself and check how you speak to yourself. If you catch yourself saying, 'You're not good enough. You're going to make a fool of yourself. You're not good at this kind of thing'. That's not going to help you. It won't support you and will take you further away from your goal. If you wouldn't say it to a friend, don't say it to yourself.

  - Once you're in a positive mindset, it's time to start preparing for the event. So many people skip this step, but uncertainty breeds self-doubt. There are a couple of pointers to consider when doing your research. The first one is – 'Is there a theme?' Some networking events do have a theme, and that theme will dictate the meeting format and subsequent conversations that take place. Does the event follow a particular format? Formats can differ considerably – some are more informal and relaxed, whereas others are more structured.

Do you have to stand up and introduce yourself to the group, or can you mingle more freely with other attendees?

- There is a lot of information about networking events, so conduct some research to see if your question has already been answered. If you can't find what you need to know, contact the event organiser and ask. Feeling uncertain and unprepared will lower your confidence and increase your self-doubt.

- The next thing to think about when in the research phase is to see who else is attending. You can usually access a guest list or see who else is posting (or being tagged in a post by the event organiser) about the event. Contact other attendees on LinkedIn or similar beforehand to let them know you're going too. Recognising a friendly face at the event will help calm your nerves.

- If attending an industry-specific event, research the latest industry trends, as these will often be a point of discussion. You don't want to find yourself in a group of people being asked your opinion about something and not knowing what they're talking about, as this will just knock your confidence.

- Finally, consider the event logistics. If you're nervous about attending and walk in late, you'll feel all eyes are on you. Arriving early has the added benefit of fewer people being in the room, so it won't feel as overwhelming.

- Be yourself

  - Approach networking with authenticity. People appreciate genuine interactions, and authentic relationships are much more likely to be sustainable and beneficial. If you are authentically you, you will attract your 'kind of people' and have a much better time. By being yourself, you'll find people will like you for you.

- When in the room, try to be approachable. Seek out anyone who is standing on their own. They might not know anybody and could feel awkward – speak to them. That's a great starting point. They'll be so pleased you've come over and want to chat with you. And don't forget to be approachable yourself. I have a bad habit of going on my phone to distract myself when feeling nervous. But that's the worst thing you can do at a networking event. Put the phone away and look up. Make eye contact, smile, and use friendly, open body language. Make it easy for people to come over to you.

- Be open-minded about who you approach. It's good to identify individuals or groups that align with your goals. But it's also really important to diversify and not limit your network to people like you, or people in your immediate field. So, try to reach out to individuals from diverse backgrounds and industries who have had different experiences because that diverse network will provide fresh perspectives and unexpected opportunities.

- Focus on building meaningful relationships rather than just collecting several contacts because quality connections are more likely to lead to valuable opportunities and collaboration.

- It's all in the follow-up
  - Make sure you regularly take time to recognise your efforts and achievements and build a system whereby you do this on a daily, weekly, and monthly basis rather than only ever congratulating yourself when you get that external validation from somebody else. Self-congratulating is the best way to maintain and build confidence.

  - Every day you will do things – sometimes big, sometimes small. You have to intentionally carve out time to recognise yourself. If you're worried about going to a networking event and it's massively outside of your comfort zone, but you push yourself to attend anyway, that's a huge achievement. So, regardless of how it went or what outcomes you got, you turned up when you could have quite easily stayed home. Acknowledging your efforts and results is key to confidence building.

- And finally, protect time after the event to interact with other attendees. You have to block time out in your diary to do this because if you don't, you'll go back to work, time will pass, and when you finally reach out, too much time will have passed, and it will feel awkward. So, protect that time after a networking event to connect and reach out to the people you've met. Send them a message telling them that you enjoyed meeting them. If there's somebody there that you were hoping to meet but didn't get a chance, message them and say that you were disappointed you didn't get a chance to chat, and you hope to meet them next time.

- End the message to your new connections with an open question to encourage conversation. An example question could be, 'What did you think of the session?' Bonus points if you can share something of value with these new connections – perhaps an introduction to someone you know could be a valuable connection to them, or a helpful resource or article related to your conversation at the event.

- Consider how you can be a valuable connection before attending any event. You don't want to turn up to a networking event and go home without having made any genuine connections. You want to connect with people and build relationships with them moving forward.

So there you have it, a guide to navigating the world of networking without the dread of walking into a room full of strangers.

Networking is about sharing who you are and what you aspire to do with your immediate circle and beyond. It's about being genuine, stepping out of your comfort zone, and embracing the power of connection in all its forms, from formal to casual chats during a jog.

Networking is a two-way street that requires giving as much as you receive. It's about being visible, vocal about your aspirations, and open to forming new relationships. The advice from successful women like Rebecca Newenham and Leanne Cooper not only demystifies networking but also shows its immense potential in fostering career growth and business opportunities. They've proven that with a bit of preparation, authenticity, and the willingness to put yourself out there, networking can go from a daunting task to an empowering tool that opens doors to endless new possibilities. Remember, it's not just about collecting contacts but building meaningful connections that can lead to mutual growth and opportunities. So, put on those big girl pants, be the person you'd love to meet, and dive into the networking scene with confidence, curiosity and an open mind.

Summary

Embrace Networking in Various Forms: Networking isn't limited to formal events; it can occur anywhere, from local community groups to informal corporate meet-ups. It's about being open to sharing your career aspirations and business goals in a range of settings.

Authenticity and Openness: Successful networking is grounded in authenticity and both giving and receiving. Share your goals and what you're looking for, but also be ready to listen and see how you can help others.

Preparation and Approachability: Prepare for networking events by researching attendees and industry trends. Approach events with the intention of being genuine and helpful. Arriving early can reduce anxiety and make it easier to start conversations.

Follow-Up Is Key: It's crucial to follow up with new contacts promptly after networking events. Acknowledge your efforts, protect time for post-event interactions, and aim to provide value in your follow-ups to nurture meaningful connections that will hopefully serve you for years to come.

Notes

1. Investing in Women (2024). How to Network Effectively to Advance Your Career. https://investinginwomen.co.uk/networking-strategies-for-introverts. Accessed 5 August 2024.
2. Investing in Women (2024). Connect with Confidence: Strategies for Effective Networking. https://investinginwomen.co.uk/networking-confidence-strategies-effective-connections. Accessed 5 August 2024.

Chapter 11

Job Interviewing

Well done, you. Your wonderful CV – or fabulous LinkedIn profile – has secured you a job interview. First of all, pat yourself on the back – the interviewer thinks you have the skills and experience for the job. An interview is your chance to highlight these skills and show you are the right person.

Now, I know that interviews can be nerve-wracking. The good news is that by spending time preparing for an interview (and the questions you are likely to be asked) now, you'll calm your nerves and be more likely to get the job. As a recruiter, I've helped thousands of candidates prepare for their interviews. I give them lots of hints, tips, and advice on how to shine and showcase their best qualities. Now, I'm bringing you my ultimate guide on preparing for YOUR interview and landing your dream role.

Company Research

When I worked as a recruiter at one of the Big 4, we always asked candidates why they wanted to work for us. This question tests how much you know about the company and what research you have done. Candidates who demonstrated that they had researched the company were more likely to get the job than those who answered, 'Because you are one of the Big 4'. This answer was too generic and one most people would know without having done any in-depth research.

So you're probably thinking, 'OK – I know I should be doing some research... but what research should I be doing?' Well, fear not – I'm here to tell you exactly what interview research to do.

- Visit the company website. You'll get a feel for the company culture and what's important to them by reading its 'about' and 'sales' pages, mission statement, new initiatives, etc.

- Run the company name through Google News. Have they been in the news recently? If so, why? Have they had any recent big client wins? These are great things to mention in the interview, and they show you've done your research!

- Who are their competitors? How do they fit within their market? These are things for you to consider. By researching the business's competitors, you can enthusiastically explain to the hiring manager why you want to work for their company over and above anyone else.

- Visit their LinkedIn company page. Here, you will see their recent updates, initiatives and current employees. Again, you can see what is important to them and get an insider view of the types of people they would like to hire. Perhaps you know one of their current team? Give yourself a headstart by getting in touch with them to see what the culture is like and the type of individuals they like to hire. Whilst on LinkedIn, have a look at your interviewer's profile. You can see their background and career history. Knowing where they previously worked, or the university they attended, means you can try to build a rapport. For example, you might know their former employer, and maybe even somewho works or worked there. If so, saying something like 'I see you used to work at X. I know [name], who worked there. They said it was a great workplace', could give you an advantage.

114

Flex

Even if you don't know your interviewer's former employer or colleagues, be sure to visit the company's other social media accounts. This will give you more material to refer to in your interview, making you look knowledgeable and keen.

Don't forget to check out any customer or partner stories you might be able to find. This can be helpful for understanding how a company's products and services are used in the real world and the feedback/reviews they've received. This helps you to see (and therefore talk about) the wider ecosystem the company operates in.

Plan for Possible Interview Questions (and Answers)

Read through the job description. What are the key skills and experience asked for? Now, think of examples where you have demonstrated these skills in your own life and previous roles.

Here are some examples of questions you could be asked:

- On the job description: Must be able to use your own initiative.
  - Possible interview question: Could you discuss a time when you recognised a problem or opportunity at work and took the initiative to address it independently? Please explain the situation, your thought process in identifying and tackling the issue, and the outcomes or improvements that resulted from your actions.
- On the job description: Must have excellent IT skills.
  - Possible interview question: Could you describe your experience with various IT systems and software? How have you adapted to new updates or changes in these systems? Additionally, could you share how you approach learning new technologies? What strategies do you use to enhance your proficiency, and how much do you enjoy this aspect of your role?

- On the job description: Provide analytical and well-documented reports to update the team on project progress.

  - Possible interview question: Could you tell us about a time when you were responsible for preparing an analytical and well-documented report to keep your team informed about a project's progress? Please include how you gathered and analysed the data, the challenges you faced, and the impact your report had on the project's subsequent phases.

Many interviewers use competency-based interview questions. A competency-based question requires you to provide real-life examples of when you have demonstrated specific skills. A competency-based question could look like this:

- Describe a situation where you had to manage a difficult stakeholder. How did you go about improving the relationship?

OR

- Give us an example of when you had to make a difficult decision. What did that process look like? What was the outcome?

The best way to answer competency-based questions is to use the STAR technique, which I've referred to throughout this book. The STAR technique requires you to refer to a challenging Situation, elaborate on the Task you undertook to overcome the challenge, what you Achieved and perhaps most importantly – the Result.

Using the STAR technique you should structure your answers following this format: what was the problem, YOUR role (sorry, not your team's role – we're not interviewing your team, we're interviewing you, so lose the 'we did this, we did that' that makes it hard for us to assess your individual contribution), and the outcome? If the result saved time or money, let us know! We love it when outcomes can be measured!

Top Tip

Keep your answers concise, and make sure you listen to and answer the actual question. Many candidates are rejected because they don't answer the questions asked. Instead, they give answers to questions they wish had been asked or ramble, taking too long to get to the point!

Why You?

Think about why you want the role. You will be asked this question! Use the job specification to emphasise your transferable skills and experience and that you have the qualities the recruiter needs. Stress how the position aligns with your future goals. Research the career paths that those who have done this role typically follow (which you'll hopefully see from your LinkedIn research) to demonstrate your ambitions and passions.

The interviewer may ask you what your strengths and weaknesses are. Candidates typically find it easier to talk about their strengths, but talking about your shortcomings demonstrates self-awareness. When discussing your weaknesses, explain how you are trying to improve on these. For example: 'I can sometimes be a bit of a perfectionist, meaning certain tasks take longer to complete. However, I am trying to set time limits for each task so I don't spend too long going over the same thing and neglect other work.'

Another question you could be asked is, 'Where do you see yourself in five years?' By asking this question, the interviewer is testing to see if you view yourself as a long-term hire. Answer by connecting your professional goals to the skills and goals you hope to gain from the role. You can also refer back to the career paths others who have previously done your role have followed.

Top Tip

If you don't know the answer to a question, be honest. The worst thing you can do is lie. Assuming the interviewer knows the answer, you will come across as untrustworthy or incompetent if you answer incorrectly. If you don't know the answer, just say. Follow this up by saying that you will find the answer after the interview. Offering to find the answer makes you look proactive and enthusiastic.

Practice, Practice, Practice

They say that practice makes perfect. In this case, it's true. Recruit your mum, dad, boyfriend, dog (actually, perhaps not that one) to act as the interviewer. Get them to ask you some typical interview questions and practice your answer to them. The more you practice, the more comfortable and, in turn, confident you will become with your answers. Ask for feedback so you can improve before the big day. If you don't have anyone to practice with, record yourself answering some typical interview questions on your phone and play them back. Objectively assess how well you've answered each question and improve from there.

Plan Your Route (or Tech)

First impressions count. The guaranteed way to make a wrong first impression? Arrive late. Aim to arrive at least 15 minutes early for a face-to-face interview and 10 minutes early for a virtual interview.

Plan your route or test your tech beforehand. For a virtual interview, make sure everything is working (laptop charged, Zoom dial-in correct, web camera on, etc.). Ensure you have a plain, neat background and are in a light room. A messy background in a dark room does not show you in the best light – excuse the pun. You can also purchase a cheap ring light to brighten up your face when talking on screen. Small tweaks like this can make a huge difference – you'll look better, which in turn will make you feel better and, therefore, more confident. A great recipe for a standout interview.

If attending a face-to-face interview, plan an alternative route should the worst happen and you get stuck in traffic. By factoring in extra time, you will cover yourself for any eventuality.

What Shall I Wear to My Interview?

Unless you are interviewing for a super-creative agency, stick to smart business attire. This is still the case (at least on your top half) for a Zoom video interview. Business attire would be a suit and tie for men. Women should wear smart business clothes, ideally with a jacket. No joke – I have known a candidate rejected at an interview because he didn't wear a tie. The interviewer felt this gave the impression he couldn't be bothered. Clothes speak a thousand words! And an interview is the time to play it safe just in case.

Is There Anything I Should Take to an Interview?

Take a pen and notebook to the interview to make notes on the role and company. (Remember, an interview is a two-way street. You're interviewing them as much as they are interviewing you!) Bring two or three copies of your CV. You should keep one for yourself and give one to the interviewer. You can occasionally refer to examples on your CV when answering questions during the interview.

Bring along a map so you don't get lost. Take the interview confirmation so you don't forget your interviewer's name!

Put all of the above in a waterproof folder in case of rain. You don't want documents getting wet and soggy.

Do You Have Any Questions for Us?

I can guarantee this will be the final question of your interview. DO NOT SAY NO TO THIS QUESTION. Remember, an interview is a two-way street. Use this opportunity to find out as much as possible to determine if this position is right for you. Asking some questions will also make you look keen and enthusiastic. It also enables you to learn more about the organisation and job you are interviewing for and whether it is the right fit for you.

So – what questions should you ask?

Here's my quick guide to the best questions to ask your interviewer at the end of your interview:

1. What will I be doing on a typical day?

The interviewer may have explained this to you during the interview, but ask if they haven't or if you're unclear. You want to clarify your daily responsibilities, as they will take up most of your time. Job descriptions aren't always clear, so this isn't a silly question. By clearly knowing what deliverables are expected, you can manage your expectations.

2. What are the most challenging aspects of the job?

Again, knowing the answer to this question allows you to manage your expectations!

Unfortunately, not all days will be easy, and no one loves their job 100% of the time, but knowing what parts of the role are most challenging will help you determine whether it aligns with your skill set and desires.

It also demonstrates to the interviewer that you have a realistic awareness of working life and are happy to meet particular challenges.

3. Why did the person previously doing the role leave?

The answer to this question may expose a red flag or reassure you. If it was an internal move, then great – the organisation retains, develops and promotes talent. If the previous person left because they didn't get on with their boss, didn't feel challenged in the position, or were not granted their flexible working request (for example), those should be warning signs that the organisation has a poor company culture or the role is unchallenging.

4. What is the company culture like?

Some of the best jobs I have had had less to do with the role itself and more about working with a great bunch of people. And I think this is the same for others, too.

Therefore – what will your colleagues be like? Will you get on with them? Will you fit in with them and ultimately want to spend up to 40 hours a week with them?

This question gives the interviewer an excellent opportunity to sell the organisation and tell you what it stands for and its values. You can then decide if your values, which you identified in Chapter 1, align with theirs!

5. How does this role fit within the team/department/company?

This question allows you to gauge your level of responsibility and the hiring manager's expectations. Who do you report to in the company hierarchy? Do you have any direct reports? How many? Do you have budget or revenue responsibility for your team/department, etc.?

6. How can I develop in the role? Do you provide learning and development opportunities?

I personally feel that a company that doesn't invest in its staff doesn't think highly of its employees and develop their talents. These types of organisations will hold people back from achieving their full potential. So, you want to know exactly how much training is available and why. Do they encourage progression and learning and development to go along with that? If not, you may become bored with the job and look for a new position sooner rather than later – and, being honest, too many short work stints on a CV is never a good look.

This question also demonstrates that you are committed to the organisation and see yourself as a long-term hire – always a plus, as no business wants to hire someone who will leave after three months (unless it's a contract role).

7. What is the typical career path for someone who has done this role?

Refer back to Chapter 1. What are your long-term career goals? Does this role help you meet them? Your answer will inform you whether the organisation offers career progression and promotes from within and whether this is the job for you.

8. How should I impress you in the first three months? How will my performance be measured?

This is a great question to ask. It makes you look keen, enthusiastic and a team player. Listen to the interviewer's response to better understand their expectations of the role and know which areas to focus on first.

9. Do you have any hesitations about my application?

I love this question, as it allows you to address any of the interviewer's concerns about your experience there and then – and gives you the opportunity to reassure them of your ability to do the job.

10. Where is the organisation hoping to be in five years?

By asking this question, you demonstrate that you see yourself as a long-term hire who wants to progress and con-tribute to the company's success.

But you also want to check if their plans align with yours. Are they planning to sell? If so, where will that leave you and your role? Or perhaps they want to grow? Again – does that mean more responsibility and opportunities for you? And is that what you want?

11. What do you enjoy most about your job?

Everybody loves chatting about themselves and their experiences. And the answer will prove insightful. You may get a more candid response about the company culture and values and how the organisation values its staff.

12. What are the next steps in the process?

This question allows you to manage your expectations regarding when you will hear back and if you need to have any more interviews.

It's an excellent neutral question and naturally draws the interview to a close.

I know interviews can be nerve-wracking, and many candidates approach them with dread, but they are a two-way street. It's good to view them as a first date rather than an audition!

You want to know if the company and role are right for you, too! Can you be yourself and flourish in the organisation? Asking insightful questions and listening carefully to the answers will allow you to assess whether the position suits you. And, if you get several job offers at the end of your job search, these responses will enable you to confidently pick the best opportunity for you – and your long-term career.

How Should I End the Interview?

Thank the interviewers for their time. Follow up with a thank-you email to the interviewers (and the recruiter if they organised it) within 24 hours of your interview. This is polite and demonstrates your enthusiasm for the role. Not everyone does this. By making an effort to send a thank you, you set yourself apart from the other candidates.

Now, it is a waiting game to see if you have got the job. Don't be too disheartened if you get a call saying you've been unsuccessful. We've all had our rejections (I bet even Bill Gates didn't get every job he interviewed for!).

The best thing you can do in this situation is to ask for honest feedback. By knowing which areas you fell down on, you can improve for next time. Sometimes, a company will hire an internal candidate if they feel they will hit the ground running quicker. Other times, it may be because you drank a 2-litre bottle of coke throughout the interview (true story – one of my candidates did that at the interview; they were subsequently rejected). Whatever the reason, it's good to know. Keep your chin up and keep applying. You'll get there – I promise. If they offer you the job, that's fantastic news – congratulations! Now, it's time to negotiate your salary and package!

Case Study – Investing in Women

My own recruitment company, Investing in Women, recently hired a marketing manager. We had over 100 applications. Here's what the candidate we chose did to stand out and ensure she was the one who was hired:

Cover Letter: The applicant wrote a personalised cover letter that demonstrated she had researched the company, detailing her experience and achievements, highlighting what she could bring to the role. It was written in a chatty and friendly style which mimicked the brand voice we use within our own business, further demonstrating her fit for the position.

First-Stage Interview: During the first-stage interview, the applicant was able to demonstrate that she had researched the company through her answers and was able to give good examples of the impact SHE had made in previous roles. There was no 'we did this', 'we did that', so we could instantly see the value she would bring to the company.

Final-Stage Interview: Before her final-stage interview, the applicant sent over a slide deck of her previous work and a mock-up of social media posts she would produce for our company. No other candidate did that, instantly helping her to stand out. During the interview, the applicant mentioned that she had already run an SEO report on our company, telling us our score and what she would do to improve it if hired. Afterwards, she followed up with a three-month plan on what she felt her priorities would be to meet the vision for the role and company, alongside some more mock-up posts. Again, no one else did this. In doing so, she not only ensured she stood out and demonstrated she could do the job, but also that she could use her own initiative and hit the ground running. This ultimately made her the obvious choice for the role.

So, have a think what YOU can do to demonstrate how you will be able to add value from day 1! What can you do to show you've done your research before, during and after the interview. And don't forget to follow up with an email and specific ideas after your interview about how you would do the job – the applicant we hired was the only one that did this. And while we're confident she will be great at the job, the other candidates who applied would probably be also have been able to do the job too. But the fact she went the extra mile to demonstrate her competence and enthusiasm meant that she was the one who was hired, and the other 99 weren't!

Summary

Preparation Is Key: Thoroughly research the company, its culture, recent news, and your interviewer. This not only shows your interest and dedication but also enables you to tailor your responses and questions more effectively.

Anticipate Questions: Reflect on the job description to identify key skills and prepare examples demonstrating these skills. Practice answering common and competency-based questions using the STAR technique to structure your responses clearly and impactfully.

Showcase Your Unique Value: Interviews are your opportunity to highlight why you're the best fit for the role. Use your research and prepared examples to demonstrate your suitability, ambition, and how you can contribute to the company's goals.

Ask the Interviewer Questions: Prepare thoughtful questions that show your genuine interest in the role and the company. Asking about challenges, company culture, and future plans can provide valuable insights and show you're considering the role seriously.

Don't Forget the Follow-Up: End the interview positively by thanking the interviewers for their time. Sending a follow-up thank-you email reiterates your interest and sets you apart from other candidates. If you don't get the job, make sure you ask for feedback so you know what areas to improve on next time.

Chapter 12

Video Job Interviews

The COVID pandemic has impacted all parts of our lives – including recruitment. With the rise of more remote and hybrid working and fewer in-person interactions, video job interviews are becoming increasingly common.

Video job interviews can be live (i.e. you meet the interviewer on a set day/time via Zoom or Microsoft Teams, or something similar), or pre-recorded, with questions automatically presented to you on the screen. You record your answers, which are then reviewed later by the employer (or increasingly, by an AI bot!).

Whatever interview format your potential employer prefers, it's good to practice and prepare so you can confidently be camera-ready and ace your next video job interview.

Do Your Interview Preparation as Normal

A video interview is no different from a face-to-face job interview. You'll be asked typical interview questions about your background, skills, experiences, and motivations for wanting the job. Therefore, as covered in the previous chapter, it is essential to research and prepare for your job interview so you know what research to do and the types of questions you might be asked (and which answers to give to wow the interviewer).

Test Your Tech

The best-laid plans don't always work out. If you're unfamiliar with the interview software, make sure you install it beforehand and familiarise yourself with how to work your camera, mute and unmute your microphone, adjust the volume, etc.

Also, choose a professional-sounding user name to create a great first impression.

Have a Practice Run

If possible, recruit a friend or family member to conduct a mock video interview with you over Zoom or Teams – or even as a video call on your phone. Get them to ask you some typical interview questions and ask for honest feedback – not just in terms of how you deliver your answers but also whether you maintain eye contact, smile, use open body language, are loud enough, etc.

Set the Scene

When you know you look your best, you will feel more confident. And the secret to looking good on camera is to have as much light on your face as possible. If you can, invest in a ring light that sits on your desk or clips onto your computer screen. A ring light shines a warm, flattering light directly onto your face, instantly making you look more energised. Alternatively, set up your laptop with your face facing the window for a similar effect.

If you can, do your trial interview at the same time of day that your interview is scheduled, so you know what the lighting looks like and if you need more (or less).

Top Tip

Slightly raise the computer and webcam (rest them on a box or purchase a special stand). Not only is this better for your neck, back, and shoulders, but it also means you look up slightly rather than down (a double chin is never a good look!).

Don't forget your background – a messy background may give the wrong impression – that you lack high standards and don't care for your work. Therefore, a plain wall behind you or smart shelves are best. You can also always blur the background or use a virtual background if needed (but if you go down this route, please don't use a funky background like a rainforest or beach scene – an office background is best in an interview situation).

Minimise Interruptions

Try to schedule your video job interview when you know your home will be quiet. If you live with others, let them know the time of your video interview so they can minimise the noise. If you have children, schedule your interview during school or nursery hours or when someone else is looking after them. You'll feel more relaxed and less anxious that someone will burst in – and therefore able to focus on the interviewer and questions better – and have the best opportunity to give your best answers. Avoid having a job interview in a coffee shop or co-working space where you can't control the background – or WiFi.

Dress the Part

Dress as you would do for an in-person job interview. Doing so will help you get 'work-ready' and increase your confidence. Although casual wear is becoming more common in the office, smart attire is still expected for most job interviews. You don't want to lose out to another candidate because they wore a smart shirt and you a scruffy t-shirt, and the interviewer then (wrongly) assumed this was because they wanted the job more than you.

Make Sure You Have Enough Charge

Imagine you are delivering a pitch-perfect answer, and the interviewer is lapping up your every word – they can't wait to hear what more you have to say – when suddenly your laptop dies because you forgot to charge it! Nightmare! The chemistry you have spent the past 30 minutes building is lost, and you look sloppy and unprepared.

To avoid this scenario, ensure your computer is fully charged and keep your laptop plugged in throughout the interview. Don't forget to set yourself up in a place with a good Wi-Fi signal.

'Arrive' Early

Just as you wouldn't arrive bang on 3:00 p.m. for an in-person job interview starting at 3, make sure you 'arrive' at least five minutes before your video interview.

This helps you double-check that all your technology is working as it should. Ensure that your background is clutter-free and that you haven't accidentally added any distracting backgrounds or filters.

Close Any Other Browsers, and Mute Your Phone

You can print off your CV, the job description, and some notes so you have them to hand – these can help you feel more confident, but try not to over-refer to them during the job interview itself – you want to maintain eye contact so keep looking at the camera, rather than yourself.

Build Rapport with a 'Digital Handshake'

Just as you would in a regular in-person job interview, building rapport with the interviewer is essential. People hire people, and ultimately, the hiring manager wants to work with someone they think they will get along with.

Use the first few minutes of the job interview before the interviewer starts asking questions to build common ground. Think of this as the time you would spend in the lift going to the interview room. So you could ask them how their day is going, if they had a nice weekend, etc.

Smile

Non-verbal communication is vital to any conversation. Smiling whilst listening to your interviewer and delivering your answers makes you appear more engaged, enthusiastic and friendly (see point above – the interviewer wants to hire someone they think they will get along with!).

Maintain Eye Contact

This can actually be quite hard to do on a video call and requires conscious effort on your part. It can be tempting to deliver your answers by looking at the person on your screen (or yourself) but to maintain eye contact like you would in a face-to-face meeting, you must deliver your answers to the camera. Straight away, you look more confident and trustworthy.

Don't Interrupt

This is good advice for life in general, but you will seem rude if you jump in and interrupt the interviewer. And with WiFi or mobile signal lag, it can be easy to interrupt someone just pausing rather than finished speaking. So, before delivering your answer, take a moment to ensure your interviewer has finished speaking.

Have a Backup Plan

As we all know, technology sometimes breaks – the internet can switch off, or apps can crash, often for no apparent reason. Therefore, getting the interviewer's phone number (or giving them yours) is wise, so you can continue the interview by phone if technology lets you down.

End on a High

It is essential to leave a positive first impression, as you would for a face-to-face job interview. Thank the interviewer for their time. Follow up with a thank-you email to the interviewers (and the recruiter if they organised it) within 24 hours of your interview. This is polite and demonstrates your enthusiasm for the role. Not everyone does this. By making an effort to send a thank you, you set yourself apart from the other candidates – and I have known this thank-you email to be the deciding factor on who gets the job on several occasions.

As we close this chapter on video job interviews, it's important to remember that while the medium may have changed, the core principles of a successful interview remain the same. Preparation, presentation, and professionalism are just as crucial in a virtual setting as they are in person. And by embracing the unique challenges and opportunities that video interviews offer, you can demonstrate your adaptability and tech savviness – highly valued qualities in today's dynamic work environment. With the right set-up, mindset, and preparation, you can turn any video interview into a compelling opportunity to sell yourself and your experience. Remember, each interview is a step forward in your career journey, and always a learning experience – so give it your all, regardless of the format.

Summary

> **Prepare as Usual:** Treat video interviews with the same seriousness as in-person interviews. Research the company, understand the role, and prepare answers to likely questions based on the job description.

Tech Check: Ensure your equipment and software are working correctly (and plugged in/fully charged) before the interview. Practice with a friend to get comfortable with the format and check your audio, video, and internet connection.

Professional Setting: Choose a quiet, well-lit space with a simple background. Dress professionally to signal you are serious about getting the job.

Be Enthusiastic: Use the camera to maintain eye contact, smile, and show enthusiasm. Your body language should convey your interest and professionalism.

Have a Backup Plan: Prepare for technical issues by having the interviewer's contact information handy. This ensures you can switch to a phone call if necessary.

Chapter 13

Job Offers

Y ou're now at the final point of your job search. A job offer is fantastic news. The employer may have been hiring for your role for months. They might have received 100s if not 1000s of CVs. They could have interviewed more people than they care to remember, but they have chosen YOU! It's important to remember that as you go into salary negotiations.

Many people fear asking for more money as they worry the employer will rescind the job offer. In all my years of recruiting, this has never happened. Not once! Employers expect you to ask for more money. If you settle for the first offer they've made, you could be leaving money on the table. It's also worth noting that men are much more likely to ask for more money than women. So, for all the ladies reading this – let this be your permission slip to ask for more money and start closing that gender pay gap.

But perhaps the thought of asking for more money brings you out in a cold sweat. Don't worry, friends; I've got you covered. This is where my step-by-step guide on negotiating your best starting salary comes in...

Step One – Market Research

Hopefully, you did this during your job search. But you need to have a realistic idea of how much money the type of role you've been offered generally pays so you don't undersell yourself (or ask for a completely unrealistic figure!).

You can do market research by speaking with recruiters and headhunters. They generally have the most up-to-date salary information. Plus, they often have salary guides they can send you.

You could ask people you know who do a similar job what the market rate is. This is probably more socially acceptable than asking them straight out about their salary, particularly in the UK, where people don't like to talk about money.

Finally, remember to visit Glassdoor's website to obtain one of their salary guides. Take the figures they provide with a pinch of salt, as they are always overinflated. Remember to adjust for location – London-based roles will always pay more than the regions.

Step Two – Give a Number, Not a Range

Don't be the first party to offer your salary expectations. If you mention your expectations too early in the process, you'll appear money (rather than role) motivated. However, when asked what your salary expectations are, be bold. Give an actual number, not a range. For example, if you want £50,000, say £50,000 rather than £45,000–£50,000 p.a. If you give the hiring managers and recruiters a range, they'll always offer at the lower end to try and save the business money.

The number you give should be your ideal number. That is, you would dance on the spot if they were to offer this salary! To determine your ideal number, you first need to work out what your 'settle number' would be. Your settle number is the salary you think is justified for the role, what you need to cover your living expenses (plus a bit extra for days out, savings and the odd holiday), and what you deserve to be paid based on your previous experience. Add 10% to your settle number to calculate your ideal number. Hopefully, you and the hiring managers will then be able to meet somewhere in the middle.

Step Three – Justify Your Salary Expectations

Now, I need you to refer to your CV and the notes you made when preparing for your interview. Consider your previous work experience using the STAR technique (see Chapter 7): the Situation, the Task YOU undertook to overcome the challenge, what YOU Achieved and the Result.

Make some notes – why are you special? What makes you unique? What experiences can you bring to the company that no other candidate can? By referring back to your key achievements, you can articulate this. Have you saved a previous employer time or money with a new initiative or automation? Did you win a large contract that brought in lots of extra revenue? If you've been out of work for a while, what brilliant transferable skills have you learned on your break?

Chances are you won't need to justify your salary expectations at all and will just get an 'okay', but if you do then let the hiring manager know calmly and confidently what makes you such a great hire (remember, they already know this as they've offered you the job but may need a gentle reminder!).

Step Four – Leverage

If you have other job offers on the table, let the hiring manager know. Believe me, they don't want to lose you to a competitor. They could have been hiring for your role for MONTHS! They may have a backup candidate if you turn the role down, but you're the candidate they want above everyone else! The thought of starting the entire process again fills them with dread. Recruitment is time-consuming and labour-intensive and takes individuals away from their day jobs.

Let the hiring manager know if you're walking away from a bonus with your current employer. Letting them know the sacrifice you're making to join them may encourage them to increase your job offer to compensate for a lost bonus, or perhaps offer you a sign-on bonus to sweeten the deal.

Step Five – Ask for Details of the Full Job Offer Package

Okay, so perhaps the salary in itself isn't quite as much as you had hoped for, but the company may have great benefits. Some employers offer free lunches (this adds up). Others will offer flexible hours and remote working (saving you money on a commute). Some employers provide free onsite gyms, excellent medical insurance, or the chance to gain professional qualifications. It's essential to ask what each benefit is worth – it can be quite a lot! Remember to find out what the employer pension contribution is and what you need to contribute as an employee. A final-salary pension is like gold dust!

Top Tip

If disappointed with your job offer, ask if the business can make up the shortfall with a sign-on bonus. An employer may be more willing to do this as there isn't an annual cost associated.

Step Six – Take Your Time

Don't accept a job offer or start negotiating straight away. Ask for details of the whole package and take these away to think through. Hiring managers expect you to take a few days to review and discuss the offer with friends and family. Please don't feel you have to accept it straight away.

The job offer has to be right for you. No one wants you to start and then leave shortly afterwards because you were not happy with the package after all. Remember, the easiest time to get an uplift on salary is BEFORE you start. Once you are in place, getting significant annual pay rises is much harder.

Step Seven – Timing Is Key

Think about a typical week for most people. No one likes Mondays! Therefore, you're more likely to get a negative response if you ask for more money on a Monday. If you can start negotiations towards the end of the week, when people have cleared their inboxes and are in a better mood, you're more likely to get the desired response. People want to wrap things up by Friday, so start your negotiations on a Wednesday or Thursday.

Step Eight – Remember You Are on the Same Team

Who likes negotiating? The hiring manager hates it as much as you do! Don't forget that. Remember, they could be your future boss and someone you will be working with day in and day out. To have got to this point, you want to work for them, and they want you to work for them! It is the same goal. Neither of you wants to start the process again.

Step Nine – Know When to Walk Away

If you're unhappy with the salary offered and the employer is not budging, know when to quit. The worst thing you can do is keep dragging out the negotiations. This will leave a sour taste in everyone's mouth. Respectfully thank the hiring manager for their time, walk away and look for other opportunities.

Step Ten – Get Everything in Writing

Verbally negotiating your salary is excellent, but it doesn't mean anything until the employer puts it in writing. And remember, don't hand in your notice to your current employer until you have your contract in your hands. Until you've been sent your contract, an employer can legally withdraw their job offer. I'm telling you this one from my own experience!

Remember, an employer expects you to negotiate. If you don't, you're selling yourself short and potentially leaving money on the table!

Summary

Remember Your Value: Remember, the employer chose you among all the other applicants, which means you have some leverage. Fear of negotiating should not discourage you from asking for a fair salary.

Do Your Homework: Research the market rate for your role to determine a realistic salary range. Use resources like recruitment agency salary guides and industry insights to inform your negotiations.

Be Specific with Your Salary Request: When discussing salary, offer a precise figure rather than a range. Start with your ideal number, knowing negotiations may bring it closer to your minimum acceptable salary.

Justify Your Ask: Prepare to explain why you're worth the salary you're asking for. Highlight specific achievements and contributions that demonstrate your value to the company.

Consider the Full Package: Salary is just one part of your compensation. Evaluate the entire offer, including benefits, work–life balance options, and other perks that may compensate for a lower salary.

Chapter 14

Flexible Working Requests

Before diving straight into flexible working requests, I think it's a good idea for me to clarify what flexible working is – and how it can work for you. Personally, I think that flexible working is anything that differs from a traditional 9–5 Monday to Friday in a onsite workplace. It can encompass part-time, hybrid, remote or term-time work, to name just a few options.

Here's my guide to some of the different working arrangements available:

Example	Why it's Great	What to Consider?
Part-time week: 3 or 4 full days (9:00 a.m. to 5:30 p.m.).	Allows you to focus and clear your workload during a long shift. It gives you 1–2 days off in the week to spend with family or for other commitments.	You will need to make childcare arrangements after school and during the school holidays. You may need to set clear boundaries with colleagues so you don't end up taking on too much work and working on your non-working day.

(continued)

Example	Why it's Great	What to Consider?
Shorter days: 5 days working 9:00 a.m. to 3:00 p.m.	These hours are perfect if you have school-age children. It also gives you visibility at work five days a week.	You won't have a day off during the week to catch up with other commitments. If you commute, you will also have to arrange some after-school care. Some companies won't offer term-time jobs, so you'll still need to arrange childcare for school holidays.
Job share: working a full-time role but sharing it with someone else, so you both end up working 2–3 days a week.	Perfect if your employer needs someone to work your job full time, but you only want part-time hours. There will also be less pressure to work on your non-working days as you know someone is covering the work.	The relationship you have with your job-share partner is critical. You must trust one another to work to the same standard and ensure an equal partnership.
Nine-day fortnight: 1 day off every fortnight.	It gives you the visibility of a full-time role whilst allowing some time off for other commitments.	You may still need to pay for childcare on your non-working day if it is not a regular weekly occurrence.

Example	Why it's Great	What to Consider?
Condensed hours: full-time hours, but worked over 4 days.	You receive a full-time salary and a day off once a week.	You receive a full-time salary and a day off once a week. You may need to pay for extended wrap-around childcare. Working extra long days could be tiring.
Staggered hours: full-time hours, but working a different shift (7:00 a.m. to 3:00 p.m., for example).	It enables you to miss rush hour and make school pick-up.	If you have children, someone else will need to wake them up and drop them off at school or pick them up, depending on your shift pattern.
Remote working: working from home on a full or part-time basis.	Saves you time and money on a commute.	You never leave your workplace, so switching off may be hard. You may also find it challenging to bond with your colleagues if you don't see them face to face.

Case Study – Laura Walker and Chloe Fletcher, Job-Shares and Founders of The Jobshare Revolution

Laura Walker and Chloe Fletcher are senior job sharers who most recently worked in a senior finance role at Asda and now run the job-share consultancy The Jobshare Revolution, which helps businesses and individuals implement successful job shares.

Laura and Chloe met at Asda when both were working on the finance team. They found that they had complementary working styles and got on well, but it wasn't until Chloe came back from maternity leave in a part-time role that the duo started to considered a job share; Laura was covering for Chloe on her non-working day and started to realise she knew exactly how Chloe thought and could slip into her shoes perfectly. Here's what they had to say:[1]

> 'Our plan to job share was a seed that was planted after Chloe returned from her first maternity leave, which then grew and grew over the next five or so years into a realistic plan. We found ourselves working four days each and weren't really thriving outside of work – the balance wasn't right for us. We started to crystallise a plan to job share and talked to our line manager about job sharing Laura's role. He was very supportive, and it was then left to us to formulate how our job share would work. For example, how would we structure the week, split our work, and present a cohesive front for the business? We didn't have a huge amount of knowledge about job sharing before we went into it. The only thing we knew was that we could work well together and we had complementary skills.
>
> We often talk about how a job share creates a unicorn employee you would never find in a single individual. Because we had such different backgrounds and experiences, we could offer so much more to the business. So, actually, for the company, it was a massive win.'

For those looking for a job-share partner, here's what Chloe and Laura recommend to get started:

Research Your Current Employer: See if they have any job-share policies or flexible working networks. Speak to HR or any other support groups to see if job sharing is actively promoted in your organisation.

Talk to Your Manager: So many job shares we know were actually paired up by a line manager or a leadership group that identified a couple of people with complementary skills within the organisation.

Look More Broadly within Your Network: Who do you know, both in and outside of work, who has a similar yet complementary background to you? Start having some conversations and see if there's anyone out there.

If you find someone, it's time to have a conversation to see how you get on – the relationship between the pair is critical, so make sure you understand each other and your drivers and values before you launch into it.

And once you've found your job-share partner, here's Laura and Chloe's advice for how to make your job share a success:

A job share is a partnership of equals. You've got to make sure that stays front and centre. You need to be evaluated together, with shared objectives and deliverables that you work together to deliver. If you give a job share two separate sets of objectives, there can be a natural tension between what you prioritise in the role – so you need to make sure you're working together on aligned goals.

The most important thing between the pair is that you've established trust and that you see each other as genuine partners. There's no room for ego in a job share. It's about working together for the collective good.

From a stakeholder perspective, the experience of working with a job-share pair needs to feel like they're working with just one individual – you need to manage the handover behind the scenes so that stakeholders (line managers, direct reports, external or internal customers) don't need to think about who they contact on each day – and they certainly shouldn't have to repeat themselves. An efficient handover enables this, so there is a seamless experience for customers and stakeholders.

As for that all-important crossover day, here's Chloe's and Laura's advice on how to make the most of that time together for you and your employer:

'It's vital to remember that in many job shares with a crossover day, a business pays for six days rather than five. Many employers are concerned about that because it's an incremental cost – but you can use it to create incremental value. Don't spend too long on handover – keep it tight to things you need to discuss rather than using time together for things that could have been communicated in other ways (e.g. voice notes, written notes, or shared documents). By keeping your handover time tight, you can make the rest of the day really productive! Set a high bar where you might be in the same room, doing the same thing together. If you can do this well and make the most of your time, then even though your employer is paying for 1.2 of an employee, they're getting 1.2 of value – or even more! Our experience is that you get even more from a job share than 1 FTE. There is some research which shows that a job share is up to 30% more productive than a single full-time employee. This is not just because you get double the skill set but because each individual is working fewer hours, they have more chance to fill their bucket doing things they love outside of work, and when they return to the office (or wherever you work), they're full of energy and ready to get started.'

Chloe and Laura are huge advocates of job sharing:

'We were both able to remain senior in our roles at Asda and achieve our ambitions whilst working part-time. We found it was a win–win for both us and our employer. We think more people and organisations should embrace the power of job sharing because it really can be transformative!'

Embracing a New Dawn of Workplace Flexibility in the UK

If you're UK-based, it's time to get ready because flexible working is about to go mainstream. The Flexible Working (Amendment) Regulations 2023 came into force in April 2024. How we work has been completely redefined since the pandemic. The previous Conservative government has recognised this and the good news is that there's no there's no more waiting 26 weeks to request the schedule you need. You can now make a flexible working request on your first day in a new job.

The new Labour Government is promising to go further by making flexible working the default from day one of employment with Employers required to accommodate this "as far as is reasonable'.' At the time of writing limited information about what this means for both companies and their workforce is available so do check out the most up to date information on the Department for Work and Pensions website.

Understanding the Change

As mentioned in the opening of this chapter, flexible working isn't just confined to where we work but also encompasses how and when we work. This could mean part-time schedules, compressed hours, staggered start times, or, of course, working from home.

Here's the breakdown:

- You can now make two flexible working requests within 12 months (up from one previously).

- Employers will have just two months to respond to your requests instead of three.

- Expect a consultation from your employer if they're considering rejecting your request – with their reasons why.

- You no longer have to justify how your flexible work affects your employer.

- And don't forget – you can request flexible working from day 1 of your employment.

Now, just because you can make a flexible working request from day 1 of your employment and can now make two flexible working requests per year or it may now be the default where reasonable in brackets, employers can still reject your request if they feel it doesn't align with business needs. Therefore, I want to help make your flexible working request count – and one that your employer is more likely to say a huge YES to! So, if you want to make a flexible working request in the future, the rest of this chapter is for you.

How to Draft a Flexible Working Request

When you're drafting your flexible working request, remember it's not just about what you need; it's also about how it can benefit your team and align with your company's goals. So although you no longer have to justify the effect your flexible working schedule will have on the company, it's good practice to consider it so you can overcome any objections your employer may have. Tom Stenner-Evans, an employment lawyer and partner at Thrive Law, suggests presenting a well-thought-out plan, anticipating potential concerns your employer might have, and proposing practical solutions. Show how your desired schedule can maintain or improve productivity, communication, and quality of work. You could also highlight the mutual benefits of flexible working: enhanced employee well-being, loyalty, and a broader talent pool.

Laurie Macpherson, a renowned career mentor, emphasises the importance of clarity and confidence when making a flexible working request. Here are some of her essential tips when structuring your request:[2]

Know What You Want: Before making a request, clearly understand your desired flexible working pattern. This could involve part-time hours, working from home, or staggered start times. Knowing your needs helps you formulate a persuasive request.

Present a Win–Win Scenario: When requesting flexible working, approach it as a negotiation where you and your employer both benefit. Highlight how the proposed arrangement can maintain or improve your productivity and overall work quality. Consider how it aligns with the company's goals and operations.

Be Prepared to Compromise: Flexibility can mean different things to different people. It's crucial to be open to negotiation and find a middle ground that suits your needs and your employer's.

Communication Is Key: Clear communication about your needs and the potential benefits to your employer is essential. Avoid focusing on personal benefits like cost savings; instead, emphasise the professional advantages to your employer if they say yes.

Understand the Employer's Perspective: Be prepared for a conversation about the business implications of your request. If you're proposing something unique, like working from a different location, research the legal and tax implications to make it easier for your employer to consider your request.

Formalise the Agreement: Once you reach an agreement with your employer, ensure it's formalised in your contract. This provides security and clarity for both parties, especially if there's a change in management or company policy.

Here's Sarah McMath, CEO of MOSL's, experience of making a flexible working request that her employer said yes to when her children were small:[3]

'I know it sounds weird, but my dream job it was basically waste-water. All the wastewater scientists across the whole of the business – all in one team. And it was absolutely everything I enjoyed about my job. It had a bit of the science. I know this sounds odd, but I really like sewage. It's fascinating. So it was my dream job, but it was a full-time job, and I remember thinking, well, what was I going to do now? I've got a seven-month-old and a just over three-year-old. I don't want to work full time, but this is the job I've always wanted. So, I initially saw the HR Director and asked them if they would consider me doing this in four days. And she said, "Yes, but what one day won't you be doing? What fifth of the job won't you be doing? And if you can't identify that, you need to push us to pay you for five days, even though you're working in four." So I went to my Director, took a big breath, and said, "Yeah, I want the job. I'm the best-qualified person for it, but I'm not working on Fridays, but I want to be paid full-time for it." And I said, "Look, I'll commit to you. I will always perform in the top quartile. I'll always be in 'exceeds expectations'. If I ever dip out of that, then I think it's appropriate for us to have a conversation about my working pattern. But if I'm always in that upper quartile, I don't think that's a conversation we need to have."

And I was really bolshie – and I was not really bolshie at that point – I developed that later on. But I took a deep breath, and he looked at me and said, "I'm going to have to say yes." I was like, "Okay, that's brilliant."

But he later confessed to me that the reason he said yes was because his daughter, who was exactly the same age as me, was working for a large IT firm, and had wanted to do the same thing. She'd had a baby at a similar time to me. But her boss had said no to her flexible working request. So what my director told me later was his instinct was to say, "No, we don't do that, and that's not fair. I'll have everybody want to work five days in four." So he had this internal dialogue, and then he thought, as a father, I can't say no because if I do, I'm as bad as my daughter's boss. And his daughter, interestingly, was called Lucy – same name as my daughter. He said, "You know, I'll be letting Lucy down because I'll be doing exactly what I've been listening to at home." So, for me, I think allyship. If that hadn't happened, my career would have taken a different path because I wouldn't have taken the job five days a week, and it worked for me. So, for me, I could have Fridays just being a mum… It worked. I could balance my work. I would always get home by about 5:00 p.m. I would do the evening tea. I love food; I love cooking, so I like that time with them. I did bath then book time, put the kids to bed at seven, and then I'd work for two hours in the evening.

That worked for me, that balance of being able to work flexibly. On Fridays, I could do things like mother and baby groups, meetings, gymnastics, and all the things I wanted to do with them. Then, once they were in school, I would go in and help out with reading at school on Fridays.

And actually, my husband did the same. So he had Mondays off. It worked in our heads that we were the primary carers for our children four days a week. Most of the week was either mum or dad or both of us. Once we got to the point where we could afford a nanny three days a week, that worked well because Annie, our nanny, was very different from me. She was very much more into clothes and makeup than I am. She and my daughter still have a very good relationship. My children were flower girls and an usher at her wedding, so they had a relationship with another person, which was a positive one. So for me, I don't feel like my children missed out during that period because they had mum and/or dad majority of the time.'

Jodie Mason, who was, until recently, Head of Workspace Services at Saint-Gobain, is also an advocate for asking for what you want. Here was her experience of making a flexible working request:[4]

'I feel that it's really important in any position that you have to ask for what you want… and I asked for that in part-time hours. When I returned to work, my manager was leaving, and his vacancy was going to be available, so I asked for that job, too. And I asked for it on my terms so I didn't feel like, "Oh well, he's full-time, so I'm going to have to be full-time." I sent an email to his line manager (who was the HR director at the time). And I said, "You know, I think I can do his job, and I can do his job well, and I can do it well because I'm this and I'm that. And I'm pretty sure that I can do it within 28 hours a week." And I explained how I thought I could make that work. I was really surprised when she invited me to discuss it. So we talked it through more, and I think she was just sort of gauging who I was and how I came across. She decided to offer me his position as a secondment for six months, and we'd see how I got on, so, if I wasn't getting on with it – if I found that going from peer to manager and managing a child at home was going to be too difficult – because my daughter at the time was about 18 months old. You know – you never quite know what's going to happen.

But I made lots of concessions. I did say that I would have Monday mornings off. And I would have Friday off, but I would remain contactable in an emergency. So if there was a break-down, an emergency, or a call out, or if there was something the team needed like sickness or something, I was always contactable during those circumstances, but it was not a working day in terms of "I'm available for meetings, or I'm available for being on-site." And she supported that. When I felt that I needed a few extra hours to get things done, I proposed to my manager, "You know, I think I can do a bit more, but I need to work from home for that, and I'll do it in the evening when my daughter has gone to sleep" because then I could still do a full day in the office, manage the team, deal with contractors on site and breakdowns and other maintenance things like review the service contracts and then go home, pick up my daughter, and have dinner with her. When my partner took her upstairs for a bath and bed, I would log back on, do another couple of hours of work, and use that to do the more administrational side (of my job).

So that was how I pitched it. My office time was for face-to-face things that couldn't be done remotely. My administration time was in the evening, catching up on emails and reviewing contracts. And again, my manager sat and thought about it and said, "All right, we'll try it." And then, at our next catch-up, she said, "How's it working for you?" And I said, "It's working great for me. How's it working for you?" She said, "It's going fine. I haven't heard any different." So we just kept it like that.'

If, after reading the advice in this chapter and Chloe, Laura, Sarah and Jodie's stories, you're inspired to put in your own flexible working request, you can find a flexible working request template to use at the back of this book.

A flexible working arrangement works for both parties when it strikes a perfect dynamic between your needs and your employer's requirements, paving the way for a dynamic, productive, and thriving working relationship.

Summary

Understand the Flexible Working Options Available: Flexible working goes beyond traditional office hours or remote working, offering part-time, hybrid, remote, or term-time working, among other options, catering to different personal needs and lifestyles.

Research the New Flexible Working Regulations: In the UK, the Flexible Working (Amendment) Regulations 2023, effective from April 2024, allow employees to request flexible working from day 1 of employment (and possible new legislation may make it the default), aiming to make flexible working more accessible and adaptable for everyone.

Craft a Compelling Request: When drafting a flexible working request, focus on presenting a plan showing mutual benefits for you and your employer. Highlight how your proposed arrangement can maintain or improve productivity and align with the company's goals.

Be Clear and Confident: Know exactly what type of flexible working arrangement you want and communicate this clearly to your employer. Emphasise the professional benefits and be ready to negotiate and compromise if necessary.

Notes

1. Elizabeth Willetts (2024). Beyond the 9-to-5: How Job Sharing Can Transform Your Career. *Work It Like A Mum* (podcast) 18 April 2024. MP3 audio, 47:41, www.buzzsprout.com/2046830/14899241. Accessed 5 August 2024.

2. Investing in Women (2023). How to Ask For Flexible Working. https://investinginwomen.co.uk/how-to-ask-for-flexible-working. Accessed 5 August 2024.

3. Elizabeth Willetts (2022). How to Get What You Really Want in Your Career – Top Tips from a CEO Who's Made It to the Top of Her Male-Dominated Industry – Whilst Working Part-Time. *Work It Like A Mum* (podcast) 24 November 2022. MP3 audio, 48.07, www.buzzsprout.com/2046830/11663396. Accessed 5 August 2024.

4. Elizabeth Willetts (2024). Sideways, Down, and Diagonal: Redefining Career Success and the Art of the Career Pivot. *Work It Like A Mum* (podcast) 29 February 2024. MP3, audio, 39:06, www.buzzsprout.com/2046830/14579117. Accessed 5 August 2024.

Chapter 15

Handing in Your Notice

When I was 18, I worked behind the bar of a local pub, pulling pints for the locals. Reflecting back, I probably wasn't the most conscientious of employees – I'd much rather have been out with my mates than working on a Saturday night. And the pub's landlady seemed to instantly dislike me, so my Saturday nights were pretty miserable. Knowing my friends were out having fun, I definitely had a massive dose of FOMO.

Anyhow, we used to wash the empty glasses in a dishwasher, which left the glasses very hot when you took them out. Dot, the landlady, always told me to put the clean, warm glasses at the back of the shelf when putting them away. But to me, that seemed a bit pointless when the glasses cooled down soon enough, and her process would require rearranging the entire shelf each time you unpacked the dishwasher, so I ignored her (looking back, I can see why I wasn't her favourite employee!).

One night, I'd put all the glasses away just as a customer came up for a pint. Dot reached for a glass and must have scalded herself because when she pulled it off the shelf, she dropped it, and it shattered all over the floor. She then screamed at me behind the bar in front of all the customers. I felt mortified. So my 18-year-old self went to the toilet and climbed out of the window, never to return! Apart from the next day when I sent my dad back in to collect my coat – spoiling the dramatic exit I'd planned!

As an 18-year-old in a weekend job with no responsibilities, I just about got away with leaving a job like that with no damage to my career, but if you're a grown-up, have responsibilities, bills to pay and a reputation that you want to protect, that is definitely not how to resign from any job – no matter how much you hate your boss!

If you've decided now's the time to say goodbye to your current role and leap into new adventures, you're probably experiencing mixed feelings. Leaving a job can stir up a mix of emotions – it's like leaving an old friend, with a bit of excitement and a dash of nervousness about what lies ahead. So, in this chapter, we will cover how to craft a resignation letter that allows you to exit gracefully (no climbing out of windows required), keep those bridges intact, and even possibly adorned with a few fairy lights.

Short and Sweet

Your resignation letter isn't the place for your memoirs. Keep it crisp and clear. Just a few lines stating that you're resigning, when your last day will be, the return of work equipment, and any other key information. Think of it like you would if you were breaking up with someone – it's best done with clarity and kindness, rather like ripping off a plaster.

Positivity Is Key

No matter the rollercoaster ride you had, how much you hated the office politics, or if you thought your boss was a jerk, keep the letter upbeat. Focus on the good stuff – what you learned, how you grew. This isn't the place for airing grievances or a list of 'could've beens'.

A Touch of Gratitude

It's always nice to throw in a 'thank you'. Maybe it's for the learning, the experiences, or that one time your boss covered for you when you were late. Gratitude leaves a lasting impression, and hey, the world's a small place; you never know when your paths might cross again – or who in your old company knows someone in your new workplace.

Lend a Hand

Offering to help with the transition is like leaving a parting gift. Maybe it's training your replacement or wrapping up projects. It shows you're professional and thoughtful to the end.

Proofread, Then Proofread Again

A typo in your resignation letter? Not the legacy you want to leave. Proofread it, and maybe get a trusted friend to give it a once-over, too.

Face-to-Face Is Best

Try to hand in your letter personally. It's a sign of respect and opens up the space for a proper conversation about your departure. It's like saying goodbye to a friend – best done in person, not via text.

Respect the Notice

Give the notice period agreed upon in your contract. Usually, it's one month, but it could be longer, so check your contract. It's about being fair, giving your employer time to adjust, hire your replacement and not leaving anyone in the lurch or one person with a two-person workload.

Wrapping up, your resignation letter is your exit music – it should leave a good impression, be respectful, and reflect the positive aspects of your time there. Keep it professional, grateful, and helpful, and you'll walk out that door with your head held high, your heart light, and minimal regrets. Here's to new beginnings and the exciting journey ahead!

Summary

Keep it Concise: Your resignation letter should be straightforward, stating your intention to resign, your last working day, and any essential details like returning company property.

Keep it Positive: In the letter, reflect on the positive experiences and growth opportunities the role provided, regardless of any challenges you faced during your time there.

Express Gratitude: Include a thank-you note for the opportunities, learning, and support you received, acknowledging the positive aspects of your job and the relationships you've built.

Offer Transition Support: Show your willingness to facilitate a smooth transition, whether through training your successor or concluding pending projects, demonstrating professionalism until the end.

Proofread Carefully: Ensure your resignation letter is error-free by thoroughly proofreading it. This helps maintain your professional image as you exit.

Deliver it Personally: Whenever possible, hand in your resignation letter in person, to show respect and provide an opportunity for an open discussion about your departure.

Adhere to Notice Period Requirements: No matter how much you want to leave and slam that door in their face, respect the notice period outlined in your contract to allow your employer sufficient time to find and train a replacement and ensure a seamless transition.

Chapter 16

Counter Offers

When you hand in your notice, your company will no doubt be disappointed and not just because you were a super-star employee. It's a real pain to hire someone new (and that's coming from a recruiter who's done it for 18 years!). It costs money – whether that's paying for job adverts, referral fees, or a very hefty recruitment agency fee (typically 20–25% of the hire's basic salary). Not to mention the internal recruiter's salary – and the more replacement hires a company needs to make, the more internal recruiters they need. It's time-consuming. It takes hiring managers and interviewers away from a potentially revenue-generating day job to review CVs and interview candidates. Once a new hire starts, training and upskilling them costs time and money. It typically takes six months for someone to 'learn' a job and start working at full throttle. Conservative estimates put the cost of recruiting and training a new hire at circa £30,000.

So, you can see why not many companies relish the prospect of making replacement hires (growth hires often invoke a different mindset).

In many instances, it is easier, cheaper, and much less hassle to counter offer someone to encourage them to stay in their job rather than go through the bother of trying to hire someone new.

What Is a Counter Offer?

So, what is a counter offer? It's when you hand in your notice, and your employer suddenly finds extra cash to persuade you to stay. But unless they're throwing an extra £30,000 your way, it's often more beneficial for them than you…

And here's the kicker: many of those (80% to be exact) who accept a counter offer find it doesn't solve the reasons they wanted to leave in the first place, and they're back on the jobs market in six months. A staggering 90% of those who accept a counter offer are in a new job in 12 months.[1]

But in the interests of balance, here are some reasons why a counter offer may be a good idea:

- It's easier – you get to stay in a job you know (and are good at) alongside familiar faces. There's no learning curve; you don't have to prove yourself to your manager (although they may view you suspiciously as a flight risk [and therefore less trustworthy] from here on out).
- You're paid more for doing the same job you did before, so if the only reason you were looking was to get a pay rise, then congratulations – you've now got one!
- You discover you're pregnant, and if you move employers, you won't qualify for their enhanced maternity pay.

But a counter offer doesn't:

- Remove a glass ceiling.
- Solve a long commute.
- Get rid of annoying colleagues who drive you up the wall.

So, if you get a counter offer, remember why they've offered it – not necessarily because they love you and think you are fan-flippin'-tastic (sorry to burst your bubble) – but to save them the pain and costs of rehiring. And if you want to leave a job for any of the reasons

I've just listed, however tempting the extra money might be, it won't make the issues miraculously disappear.

And remember, if they thought that much of you in the first place, they wouldn't have waited for you to hand in your notice to open their wallets!

But hey – it's your call. It's your career. You know you, your job, team and circumstances better than anyone, so ultimately, you've got to weigh up the pros and cons, think about exactly why you wanted to leave your old job in the first place, and do what's right for you. Remember – it's your career and YOUR journey.

Summary

What Is a Counter Offer? When you hand in your notice, a counter offer may come your way, offering more money or benefits to stay. However, these are often more about the company's convenience than your career growth.

The Cost of Hiring: Companies find replacing employees expensive, with costs potentially reaching £30,000 (factoring in advertising, hiring, and training). This makes counter offers a cost-effective strategy for retaining staff.

How Effective Are Counter Offers? The majority of people who accept counter offers (around 80%) start job hunting again within six months, indicating that these offers rarely address the root causes of wanting to leave.

When Should You Consider a Counter Offer? Counter offers might appeal if they directly address your main issue, such as salary. However, they won't change fundamental problems like career progression, a long commute or difficult colleagues.

Why Were You Looking for a New Job? Reflect on why you wanted to leave in the first place. A counter offer can seem tempting, but it's crucial to consider whether it truly resolves your reasons for wanting to move on.

Your Career, Your Decision: Ultimately, whether to accept a counter offer should align with what you want from your career and life. You should carefully make the decision by considering how it will impact your professional journey, personal circumstances and long-term career goals.

Note

1. Eclipse Marketing Software (2018). 7 Counter Offer Statistics Every Recruiter Needs to Know. www.recruitment-software.co.uk/7-counter-offer-statistics-every-recruiter-needs-know. Accessed 5 August 2024.

Chapter 17

Making an Impact at Work

So, you've landed your dream job. You like the company and team. You know you are now on the right career path for you, and you want to climb that career ladder and make the biggest impact you can.

But how?

When life is busy it can be easy to get caughtup in the day-to-day. You can start to feel like a cog in a machine – particularly if you work for a large corporate where you can feel like a small fish in a very large pond.

But there are ways for you to make the biggest impact you can at work, be noticed, appreciated, and respected, leading to bigger opportunities – all the while respecting your boundaries and work – life balance. In this chapter, I'm going to show you how.

Think back to Chapter 2, where entrepreneur Alex Hormozi talks about the importance of skill stacking. As a reminder, skill stacking is continuing to build on your skill and knowledge so your skillset becomes unique to you – and you become invaluable to your employer.

I can certainly attest that when I learn something new, my confidence soars, and I bring that new-found confidence and energy to my sales calls, team meetings, and general day-to-day activities. Learning something new is a surefire way to give you a boost, improve your skills and competence, and increase your motivation. Learning something new also increases your value.

The best people at work always ensure that the work they do, the experience they gain, and the skills they learn add value, enabling them to build trust, influence, and respect within their workplaces. These are all hugely positive traits we like to see in our leaders.

Roz Hobley, a leadership and performance coach, is an expert on how to build trust, influence and respect at work through what she calls the four forces: character, chemistry, competency, and credibility. Each force plays a crucial role in how you connect with others and establish your presence – and influence – at work. I asked Roz for tips on building influence, credibility and trust at work, enabling you to make the biggest impact you possibly can – and get the respect you deserve. Here's what she said:[1]

Character: The Foundation of Trust

'The first way of unlocking trust with people is through character. Character boils down to this: do you do what you say you're going to do? Do you have integrity? If you say you will do something and deliver on it, that immediately builds trust. You increase your propensity for people to be open to your judgement, opinions, recommendations and requests. And ultimately, the extent to which people trust you will determine how much you can influence them. And the legacy that each of us leaves will, to a great extent, be determined by the influence that we have positively had or shared we others.'

Chemistry: The Power of Likeability

'Likeability is part of chemistry, and it's a key element of influence. When people like you, you become more persuasive and influential – and others become more open to your ideas. But interestingly, your likeability, in part, comes from how you make people feel. You can tell how much someone likes you through body language – 93% of our communication is non-verbal. So if

you are attentive – you look at that person and are present with them – you'll gain a real sense of how much they are invested in your relationship. My top tip to make yourself more likeable is to be curious. Ask questions about people, and always have a few questions up your sleeve. For example, what's your favourite thing to do at the weekend? What's the best holiday you have been on? I recently worked with a group of lawyers and was trying to build influence in that group (and it's worth noting I do not have any personal experience in law). I wanted to show them that I knew what I was doing and appear competent. But I had to be quite honest – I do not know everything, so to build that credibility and influence with them, I made a point of being super curious. No question is a bad question. I want to learn as much as possible about them, their culture, industry and team. So, asking questions, whether in a work or social context, is great. And most of us love to be asked a good question.

Also, try to remember details about people's lives. When you ask a question, that's the first stage. Somebody gives you that information, but then take it, absorb it, work with it, and build on it. So the next time you see them, you can follow up with more questions – "How is your dog after their operation?", "How was that walking holiday," "Did so and so get that new job?" (or whatever it was). If you can have a couple of key facts or useful pieces of information in your mind that are important to that person, bring them to the fore when you meet them next. This will build a relationship because it will show that not only are you interested in that person, but you have remembered them, and you are following up.

Do not forget that 93% of our communication is non-verbal. So when you are with people, it's not just what you are saying, but being present by putting your phone away, using open body language and smiling. This shows that you are enjoying the con versation and being with them. All of this will build positive rapport and contact.'

Competency: Establishing Your Expertise

'This is how much of a track record you have in what you're doing. Are you an expert in your field? Do you have a good track record of doing whatever you do? You can build influence by showing that you really know what you're talking about.'

And continuing to learn and gain experience is the best way to build your expertise.

If you suffer from imposter syndrome, here's some of Roz's advice to feel more competent, even if you feel out of your depth:

'My first piece of advice is upskilling, whether that's finding a mentor, listening to podcasts, doing some training, reading a book and knowing what are the key materials. Think – "What would I need to read to know a bit more about this?" and then be super intentional about upskilling yourself. The second thing is the mindset, and I've got a question that I find helpful: "What relationship do you want to have with your imposter syndrome?" And for me, I want a relationship where it's there. I know it's there, but it's getting continually further away. And for it to move continually further away, I trust myself and invest in my learning. It's a choice. It's choosing not to dwell on that imposter syndrome and having a relationship where I'm pushing it further away. You can choose what relationship you want to have with your imposter syndrome and how much control you want it to have over you. And that can be an active choice every day. When you walk into the room and look the part, you are confident and full of energy and anticipation for the job; no one will know you have got it. It's only you who knows. But if you let imposter syndrome control you, you will not push yourself to try something new and instead stay static.

And, once you push past your imposter syndrome, you will get to that lovely point where you are more confident – and competent in your job.'

Credibility: Staying Relevant

'The fourth way to build trust and influence with people is through credibility. And being credible – that's about being relevant. So, if you're preparing for a job interview, it's about taking your personality, skills, experience, life experience, and knowledge, and having the ability to make it relevant to the person you're with, showing that you understand or are relevant to their world, to their context, to their challenges, and that your expertise can help them to overcome those challenges or achieve their goals.'

Like Alex Hormozi, Roz is a huge advocate of investing in yourself and your learning, so you continually upskill yourself, building your competence – and, therefore, your confidence. By purchasing this book and going through the exercises, you have taken a hugely positive first step in the learning process, but I want you to make sure you do not stop here once you get a job and life gets busy. Learning should be enjoyable and something we do our entire lives. Stay curious – none of us ever knows everything – there is always more to learn. Learning expands our horizons and teaches us new things. We discover things about ourselves in the process; it makes us more interesting human beings and prevents life from ever getting boring. It enriches our lives and allows us to add more value to all aspects of it. In short, take time to regularly invest in yourself by learning something new or building on your existing skills and knowledge. It does not have to be expensive – free YouTube videos, podcasts, and cheap self-help books are all perfect tools that you can easily access at any time of the day. But do not stop – future you will thank you for taking the time to back yourself by investing in your learning, whatever your age or the stage of your career.

How to Get Over Imposter Syndrome

I launched Investing in Women from my dining room table during my kids' nap times on an old laptop and with a £5,000 redundancy payout. Even though I had recruitment experience, my imposter syndrome was huge. I had the audacity to want to launch a job board with zero audience, no tech skills and extremely limited funds. I could see job boards being launched all around me that had raised millions of pounds worth of funding or by influencers with huge audiences. My nerves were sky-high – what if no one visited my website or posted roles? Due to said limited funds, I had to be imaginative about how I would market the business (hence all the LinkedIn Lives that I could do for free), to stand out in a sea of competition.

So, it's comforting to know that even the most successful people have suffered from imposter syndrome at some point in their lives, including Rosie Reynolds, now the Chief Commercial Officer of the investment management firm Aspect Capital.

Rosie grew up in a small village in Scotland. She attended the local comprehensive school and initially wanted to be a vet. Growing up, she did not know anyone who worked in finance, but as she got older, she decided she wanted a job that involved travel, and a career advisor at school suggested international law. So without really knowing what the role fully involved, Rosie applied to study law at the University of Glasgow, which was followed by a training contract in London where she found herself surrounded by peers who had studied at public or grammar schools and for a long time, Rosie felt like an outsider looking in.

At many points, Rosie wasn't sure she had the credentials to succeed, but she persevered, and slowly but surely, her confidence grew, and she realised that she had achieved some amazing things.

And just that reframe completely boosted Rosie's confidence. Here's what Rosie says about recognising your skills and abilities:[2]

> *'I realised that, hang on, I have achieved things. And that's really empowering. It pushes you to grow in other areas of your life. And I think that's when you become more at ease with some of the decisions that you've made, you worry less. You feel slightly more confident that you're parenting the best you can. You feel slightly more confident about what you're achieving. I can translate that into sports. I can translate that into pushing myself further in my organisation. I can have another child. I can do this! I suppose that realisation came to me quite late in my career in terms of the trajectory so far. And it's something I've only realised really in the last few years, but that's definitely propelled me further. I think imposter syndrome can be what gives you your drive. It certainly gave me the drive and ambition to keep trying and not give up.'*

Personally, I now view imposter syndrome as an essential part of building a successful career. We all get it when we step into something new – no baby can run a marathon the first time they take a step, and no child can cycle perfectly the first time you remove their stabilisers. So why would you be fully competent on your first day in a new job? It will take some time to learn how to do a new role and become fully competent – and that's okay. If you can get through that uncomfortable stage when you are learning, the growth (and confidence) you'll experience afterwards is just phenomenal. So, don't let your imposter syndrome talk you out of anything. Get comfortable sitting alongside it, recognise that it's normal and keep going! There's also a school of thought that when you are no longer feeling that imposter syndrome, you have become almost too competent and no longer growing and developing, and, therefore, it's time to move on – and up – in your career.

Making an Impact at Work

Often, it's a case of finding the right manager to support you, particularly early in your career. Rosie felt that one of her first bosses was instrumental in helping propel her career forward:

'I was extremely lucky in my training contract to have the most amazing boss and mentor, who had also gone to Glasgow University. And I suppose he spotted some potential in me – and championed me throughout my early years as a lawyer – and still does now, even though we no longer work together. He took an interest in my career and invested time in me. He gave me responsibility far beyond what I should have had, and I felt incredibly supported by him. He was a great role model; even now, I often ask myself how he would approach a particular issue. He's really the person that I would credit most with having pointed me in the direction I'm in now and given me the confidence to push ahead no matter what, to worry less about some of the ancillary issues in the background and just go for it. He has a laser focus on clients and an incredibly strong work ethic. In terms of problem-solving and thinking laterally around a problem to achieve the best outcomes for a client, his view was that challenges can always be resolved, keep going above and beyond and never give up. This is a philosophy I've tried to adopt in my own career consistently. And I credit my mentor with this; he was fundamental in instilling self-confidence in me and catalysing my career.'

So, find a champion or mentor at work – someone you admire – and see if they can take you under their wing. It's never a bad thing to make yourself visible to department managers and try to get time in their diaries. And it's been shown that those who make themselves known to their bosses' boss (in the best way possible, of course) tend to progress their career faster than those who keep their heads down and stay small. In most cases, people want to help and will be flattered by being asked to mentor you. Make sure you use your time with them intentionally – always prepare some questions beforehand, be open to their suggestions, and always thank them for their time! And do not forget to network with your direct peers as well. Many of the people featured in this book found a new opportunity at work because they were friendly, approachable, networked, and open to meeting new people and teams.

This is the basis for building great relationships in your industry and a network that will serve you for years to come.

Setting Goals, Achieving Objectives, and Getting the Recognition You Deserve!

As well as great relationships and a strong network, to achieve promotions, pay rises and great work opportunities, you need to consistently demonstrate to your employer that you are not only a safe pair of hands but that you can also add value to them and their business. To do that, you need to regularly have open and honest conversations with your manager about your role objectives, achievements and deliverables, as well as what the outcome will be if you achieve them.

So, at the beginning of each year, sit down with your manager to set measurable role objectives and goals and determine what good – and excellent – looks like. Ensure you understand what exactly you need to deliver to score highly in performance reviews. If something is measurable, it is much easier for you to demonstrate that you have/have not achieved it. And if you have achieved your objectives at the end of the year, you have demonstrable proof and a body of evidence that you have delivered and, therefore, deserve that promotion/pay rise/bonus. If you have proof that you have met an objective that was set, it is very hard for an employer to say no and turn down your request without losing face and your respect.

Career advancement coach Leanne Cooper advises her clients on the importance of advocating for themselves and their achievements if they want to progress in their careers. As she says:[3]

> *'We've got to self-promote. And as much as I'm a massive fan of flexible and remote working, you can't just sit in your home office working really hard and expect people to know what you're doing. So, unless you can promote yourself effectively, confidently communicate your contributions, and be vocal about that unique value that you're adding, you're at risk of being overlooked, experiencing career stagnation and salary disparities. If you're invisible when things are changing and decisions are being made, you risk having less credibility and less authority'* (all the things, if you remember, Roz advocates we need to have for those leadership roles)!

Leanne continues:

> *'If we don't self-promote, we miss out on promotions and are overlooked for opportunities. And I know lots of people feel nervous about self-promoting. Many of us have been raised not to show off, stay quiet, work hard and get on with it. So, it's not surprising that we find it hard to speak up for ourselves and our work. To be clear – when I say self-promoting, it doesn't mean you have to stand on your chair in the middle of the office with a megaphone in your hand, broadcasting your wins. There are other ways that we can do this effectively. Here are my tips about how to self-promote, whether you are an introvert or extrovert and office or home-based:*
>
> **Be Intentional with Your Small Talk:** *It's time to shift your mindset from thinking that self-promotion is big*

announcements and bold statements. It doesn't have to be that – it can be as simple as dropping in some of your achievements during those "water cooler" conversations, whether in real life by the actual water cooler or over Teams or Zoom. You can slip into conversations about things you're working on, who you're working with, and what you're proud of and celebrating. It can feel quite natural and is just an extension of "I'm good, thanks" when asked how you are getting on. Put some context in there and say, why are you good? And if you're proud of yourself for something you've done, don't be afraid to say. In doing that, you create a safe space for others to share their achievements and help create a nice, positive, and supportive working environment for everybody.

Review Your Achievements: *Protect time every month to review your achievements and look at where you've added value. In the day-to-day, it's easy to get caught up in doing your work. So, you have to be intentional about reflecting on what you have to show for the work you do. Make an appointment with yourself every month in your diary to look at where you've added value and quantify it as well. Don't just say that you've saved your employer money. How much money have you saved? How much money have you brought in if you're in a revenue-facing role? How many new people have you trained? How many people have you recruited? Be specific about the value and share it. You can also input that information into your CV, which helps when you're looking for a new job because otherwise you forget. It's good practice to do this for confidence building and preparing for interviews and appraisals. Don't just keep that information to yourself. Get into the habit of sharing it with your boss. Send them an email at the end of the month telling them what you've been working on and, more importantly, what you've achieved.*

Making an Impact at Work

Sharing Is Caring: *If you've created something unique that's helping you do your job, share it! Tell colleagues how it's helping you. Don't just use a fantastic tool you've created on your own; teach people how to use it. Share any helpful industry publications and white papers you've learnt with your team. There are so many ways to get front of mind with people and to show your employer that you're an authority figure and an expert in your field.*

Take Back Control of Your Career: *Waiting to see what will happen or what opportunities may come up is one of the worst things you can do for your career. You're leaving your career in other people's hands rather than making deliberate career decisions. You're lacking direction, strategy, and just hoping that somehow you will end up where you want to be by accident. You're waiting for opportunities to find you instead of creating them. So, it's essential to make a plan and stay in control. Let's say, for example, you are looking for a promotion. Ask for the job description for the role and volunteer to shadow someone doing the role. Doing this will show that you're ready for that next step. I remember years ago, I wanted to step up to be a team leader. I was in a deputy role at the time, so I sat down with my team leader and asked what I could do now that was in the team leader job description? And she said, "Well, you could start doing this task." If you do this, when that promotion becomes available, you'll be able to show you've had some exposure and experience of doing it. In your monthly review, ensure you're clear to your manager about the value you're adding and link it back to the organisation's overall goals. Look at what your organisation wants to achieve this year and link back to the work that you are doing and how you are contributing.*

Gather every single bit of feedback you've ever been given, whether it's a voicemail, an email, a text message, a letter, or whatever – gather it all. And then proactively seek some more. This will help you identify any skills or knowledge gaps that might hinder your progress into that next role and give you the chance to address them and upskill. The people who can successfully pivot or make that next step in their careers are the ones who invest some time and potentially some money to upskill, even if it's just by reading a book (like this one), watching a YouTube course or listening to a podcast.'

Case Study – Nicola Lee, Sales Manager at Jewson

Nicola Lee has worked with Jewson, the builders' merchant, for almost 30 years. She started her career with them, working in a branch. But after returning to work following the birth of her twins, something shifted; becoming a mother fuelled her ambition, and she decided she wanted to achieve even more in her career. Here was her experience:[4]

'I had this amazing moment when I returned to work after having the girls. I went back to my job as a sales coach at Jewson. I was coaching people on their sales by listening to phone calls and giving them feedback. And it was a really good job. I enjoyed it, but just thought I could do more. And I looked at the other people in the office and wider organisation and thought, you know, I think I could get a job with a bonus. I think I could get a job where I could earn more. I could be part of the senior team, trying to shape the business and where we're going.

And all I kept thinking was, I've had two babies born six weeks early. I've looked after them, and now they're thriving.

What a huge achievement I'd done with my family and husband, with the help of others around me. I had brought two humans into the world with my husband. And if we'd survived that, why could I not do more? And honestly, from that moment, I took a couple of chances. I took a job that I thought was completely different. You know, when you apply for a job, and you get it, and then you start doing it, you think, well, this is nothing like I thought it would be – I had this real sink or swim moment. But I just kept thinking, I've had these two babies – I've gone through that, and I'll just keep going. And I did, and I've really not looked back in the last 15 years.'

Nicola is now a senior sales leader, managing a team of eight direct reports. Here's her advice to others looking to get ahead in their careers – and building that trust Roz says is so vital for leaders:

'It's important to acknowledge what you know whilst also making sure you acknowledge what you don't. But rather than admitting defeat and being seen as unhelpful, say, "I'm going to find out". I think if you're upfront and honest about that, then people will respect it. And nobody's ever going to get upset or cross with you if you say, "I don't know the answer to that, but if you give me five minutes, I know someone who will". And then go away, find the answer and come back to them.

It's crucial to do what you say you're going to do. You should have that mantra almost printed inside you as you want that to be what you're known for. I've built a career building relationships and networks and having contacts. So if I don't know the answer, I'll find somebody that does. And sometimes people phone me just to say, "I don't know where else to go with this problem. So I thought I would phone you as I know you'll know someone who will be able to help". As long as you go back to them, you build that credibility.'

So, there you have it – the road to making a significant impact at work is not paved with just your skills but also with your ability to continuously learn and grow within your role – and build those all-important relationships. Whether you are in a large corporate or a smaller setting, standing out involves more than just meeting expectations. It requires building a unique set of skills, being genuinely engaged with your colleagues, and maintaining a relentless pursuit of personal and professional development. In this chapter, we have unpacked the strategies to ensure you are not only noticed but also valued within your workplace. From skill stacking and network building to mastering the art of influence through character, chemistry, competency, and credibility, each step is a building block towards not just being another cog in the machine but a pivotal part of your company's engine. Remember, every interaction and every task is an opportunity to demonstrate your value and drive your career trajectory towards even greater heights. Keep pushing the boundaries, stay curious, and let your genuine passion for your work shine through.

Summary

Skill Stack for Success: Continuously enhance your skill set to make yourself invaluable to your employer. This approach not only boosts your confidence but also ensures you remain competitive and relevant in your field.

Build Influence Through Character and Credibility: Establish trust and influence in the workplace by consistently demonstrating integrity and reliability. Show that you can be counted on to deliver what you promise, enhancing your professional reputation.

Utilise Chemistry and Likeability: Engage with colleagues and superiors through genuine interactions. Being personable and approachable increases your likeability, which can significantly boost your persuasive power and influence within the company.

Demonstrate Competence and Expertise: Prove your expertise through a solid track record and continuous learning. Stay up-to-date with industry knowledge and be prepared to tackle challenges competently to elevate your status as an expert.

Embrace Lifelong Learning and Seek Opportunities for Professional Development: Whether through formal education, mentorship, or self-study, expanding your knowledge base and skills is crucial for career advancement.

By following these strategies, you can ensure that you make a significant and recognised impact at your workplace, paving the way for advancement and success.

Notes

1. Elizabeth Willetts (2024). From Self-Awareness to Success: Mastering Influence at Work with Roz Hobley. *Work It Like A Mum* (podcast) 7 March 2024. MP3 audio, 39:12, www.buzzsprout.com/2046830/14624517. Accessed 5 August 2024.
2. Elizabeth Willetts (2022). 'I felt like an imposter for a long time in my career – now I'm the COO of a leading Asset Management firm'. *Work It Like A Mum* (podcast) 1 December 2022. MP3 audio, 47:09, www.buzzsprout.com/2046830/11756406. Accessed 5 August 2024.
3. Elizabeth Willetts (2024). From Invisible to Invincible: Self-Promotion Strategies for Career Success. *Work It Like A Mum* (podcast) 9 May 2024. MP3 audio, 31:58, www.buzzsprout.com/2046830/15024303.
4. Elizabeth Willetts (2024). Want to Thrive in Your Career After Kids? Here's How One Woman Crushed It (And Even a Cancer Diagnosis Hasn't Stopped Her). *Work It Like A Mum* (podcast) 21 March 2024. MP3 audio, 41:33, https://www.buzzsprout.com/2046830/14732476. Accessed 5 August 2024.

Chapter 18

Asking for a Pay Rise – and Getting Paid What You Deserve!

Negotiating a pay rise can be daunting, but it's an essential skill that can significantly benefit your career, financial well-being, and security. Particularly as, unfortunately, so many employers base a new hire's job offer on their previous salary. You don't want to get caught in a cycle where you are underpaid, as it's one you may never get out of. Whether you're looking to negotiate a raise with your current employer or a new job offer, there are several key factors to remember.

Research the Market

Before negotiating your pay, it's essential to research the current market rates for your position and industry. This will help you manage your expectations and give you leverage in your negotiations. You can use salary comparison websites, industry reports, and job postings to better understand what others in similar roles are earning.

Highlight Your Value

Highlight your achievements and contributions to the company. Be specific about how your work has positively impacted the business – ideally through metrics, whether it is increased revenue, cost savings, or improved processes. This will help your employer understand your worth and why you deserve a raise.

Timing Is Key

Timing is everything when it comes to negotiating a pay rise. Consider the company's current financial situation, as well as any recent changes or challenges. Negotiating a pay rise during a downturn or after a round of redundancies will be more difficult. Similarly, it may be easier to negotiate a raise after a particularly successful project or when the company is experiencing growth or record revenue.

Practice Your Pitch

Before you meet with your employer, practice your pitch. Be clear and concise about your reasons for requesting a pay rise and why you think you deserve one. Be prepared to answer any questions or objections that may arise. Consider role-playing with a friend or family member to help build your confidence and refine your pitch.

Be Open to Compromise

Negotiating a pay rise is a two-way conversation, and it is vital to be open to compromise. If your employer cannot meet your salary expectations, consider other forms of compensation, such as bonuses or commissions that only reward you if you deliver on certain agreed targets (less of a risk to your employer and more of an incentive to you), additional annual leave, flexible working hours, or professional development opportunities.

Follow Up

After your meeting, follow up with your employer to confirm any agreed-upon terms. If the negotiations are unsuccessful, make sure you ask why and if any targets could be set that, if you hit them, would mean a pay rise in, say, six months. That way, you know what you are working towards, making it a lot more difficult for your employer to say no next time if you do deliver. And if you do deliver and hit those targets and you're turned down again, then you know that this isn't the employer for you, and you can start looking elsewhere.

In conclusion, negotiating a pay rise can be challenging, but it's an essential skill that will significantly benefit your career and financial well-being. By researching the market, highlighting your value, timing your request, practising your pitch, being open to compromise, and following up, you can increase your chances of getting the pay rise you deserve.

Summary

Do Your Research: Understand the market rates for your position within your industry so you enter discussions with realistic expectations and strengthen your negotiating position.

What's Your Value Proposition: Clearly articulate your contributions and achievements, using specific examples and metrics to demonstrate how you've positively impacted the company.

Timing Is Key: Choose the right moment to discuss a pay rise, considering the company's financial health and your recent performance.

Practice Makes Perfect: Practice your negotiation pitch to confidently and succinctly present your case for a pay increase and the value you have brought your employer, preparing for potential questions or pushbacks.

Compromise: Be ready to negotiate alternative forms of compensation if a direct increase in salary isn't feasible, such as performance bonuses, extra leave, or training opportunities.

It's All in the Follow-Up: Confirm any agreements in writing and understand the reasons behind any refusal. If appropriate, negotiate specific targets for future evaluation, which can help in securing a raise down the line.

Chapter 19

Starting Your Own Business

Sometimes, the best course for your career is to work for yourself. This may be because of the flexibility being self-employed can bring – no needing to ask the boss for a day off to attend your child's sports day, for instance. You may prefer the variety of work you can do running your own business and the fact that there is no ceiling, or you may just have an inkling of a business idea you want to put out there.

There are lots of routes to self-employment, including freelancing, becoming a contractor, setting up a franchise, and, of course, starting your own business.

While this is not a business book – there are many excellent books on sale that offer advice on how to run a successful business – thanks to the internet, it has never been easier to work for yourself or launch a business with minimal outlay. Many people have launched successful businesses from home, around family commitments, after a career break, or monetised a hobby.

But before ditching your 9–5, remember, going down the self-employment route is risky. There is no guaranteed salary, and if, like me, you started a business for flexibility around family, you may find yourself working more hours than you'd have ever done in an employed role working for someone else! So before purchasing that web domain, here are some things you should consider first.

What Do You Want?

Revisit Chapter 1 – what are your strengths, values and definition of success, and how does this align with your business goals? Is running the next Amazon your idea of business heaven, or would you be quite happy working as a freelancer during school hours? Do you want a product-based business, or is selling services more your thing? Do you want to work outside the home, or is tapping away at your laptop from the kitchen table the dream? Would you like to work with lots of different clients – or just a few? And talking of clients, who is your ideal client? Is it other businesses or individuals? Would you like to start something from scratch that is uniquely yours or buy an established business or franchise with proven systems, frameworks and a track record?

The answers to these questions will help you define what your ideal business looks like, how it will work in practice, and whether it's right for you.

What Can You Do?

What skills and experiences have you gained during your life, and if you are launching a service-based business, what will clients pay for? Are you good at admin? How about becoming a virtual assistant? A numbers person? What about becoming a bookkeeper? Do you like working with children? How about running children's classes in your local community centre? Or do you see a gap in the market and would love to develop a product that will fill it?

Consider who you are beyond your skills. What are you like as a person and what do you enjoy doing? Are you a people person or prefer working alone? These questions should help you narrow down the business structure that will suit you best.

Case Study – Amanda Henderson, Freelance HR Professional

Amanda is a seasoned HR professional who left the corporate world and opted to return to work freelancing after the birth of her second child. Here's how Amanda's freelancing journey began:[1]

'I'd just completed my Level 7 CPID when a client approached me to do an interesting contract for them on a freelance basis, and I just got a real taste for it. I enjoyed the work so much. It allowed me to apply all my operational skills and experience in an HR context. That first contract led to a second, and I was about four months away from going back to work, and it just became a now-or-never sort of thing. I had a safety net to some extent because the pandemic had changed the jobs market so much that I was relatively sure I would be able to find employment again doing what I did before.

To get my freelancing business off the ground, I spent time messaging a lot of people in my network through LinkedIn, sharing what my new business could offer. I was fortunate to have spent a lot of time building my network on LinkedIn in the years before going alone. And those messages got the ball rolling and helped me get my early clients.

When I first started, I made the terrible error of working out my day rate based on my salary. This is a massive fail from a contracting perspective because, as a contractor, you are saving an employer the associated costs of employing someone directly (Employers' National Insurance, for example), as well as taking a lot of the risk (no holiday pay, sick pay, etc.) to enable that company to reduce its own financial liability and commitments.

So, *don't work out your day rate based on your current or most recent salary. To give you an idea of how wrong I had it, my day rate is now about three times where I started with it! Obviously, I have gained more recommendations and experience, but I've also gained more confidence – confidence I should have had starting out when I'd already had lots of valuable work experience.*

When I started my freelancing business, I invoiced at the end of the month. I don't know why, but I used to offer clients 30-day payment terms, which, looking back, was crazy. It meant I'd do the work, say in January, but wouldn't be paid until March (and that's if they actually paid on time)!

I also stupidly didn't have any late payment charges or agreements in my early SLAs (service level agreements) around "downing tools" if I wasn't paid, which was a huge mistake. Very early on, a client went AWOL with an unpaid invoice for £1,500, which was a lot of money to me when I was just starting out.

But I learned from that. I now have robust SLAs in place and am confident in enforcing the wording. All retained clients now pay for my services upfront and have just 7 days to pay their invoices. If they don't, that's it – I pause working for them until it is paid.

Despite all the learnings and occasional pain points, I don't regret jumping into freelancing one bit and am very proud to run Thread HR. It has given me such a breadth of experience very quickly as I've worked on an enormous range of projects. If I'd stayed in corporate, I think I would have been limited by recruiters because I didn't have the job titles HRBP or HR Director on my CV, but in fact, doing my own thing has allowed me to steer my course and get more meaty roles that utilise my skills. I feel very lucky to be in that position.'

Flex

Is There a Market for Your Business?

Do not – I repeat, *do not* – skip this step. The advice if you 'fail to plan, plan to fail' never felt more apt than when considering whether to start a VIABLE business – yes, *viable*.

Are there already potential competitors operating in your market? If yes, do not feel threatened – this is actually a good thing as it demonstrates there is a market for your business. But who are your potential competitors, and how can you differentiate your business from them? What will be your unique selling point that will tempt customers to try your product or service over theirs?

And if there is not already a market for your product or service – why not? Have other businesses tried and failed? If so – why? Is there something you can do differently?

Do your market research. Who will be your ideal customer? Do they want your offering? How much are they willing to spend (and will that amount cover your costs)? Where do these customers 'hang out' on and offline? And how will you reach them to tell them about your product or service?

What Business Structure Suits You?

There are lots of ways you can structure your business, including becoming a sole trader, forming a partnership, or setting up a limited company. The best business structure will depend on the type of business you want to run and how large you want it to grow. Get advice from an accountant and, for those based in the UK, do not forget to visit the Companies House website for further guidance.

How Much Should You Invest?

I'm a big believer that during the early days you want to invest as little money as possible while you test to see if there is a market for your product or service. You do not want to invest in fancy premises if you can initially run your business from a Shopify website at home while you test your product, make the mistakes you will inevitably make in your first year of business, and possibly pivot your business into something else. As you prove your business concept by making sales and profit, you can add more fancy funnels, a swish premises, or an upgraded website later on, once you have proof of concept.

But there will be some things you need to get your business off on the right foot, including:

- **A Website to Act as a Shop Window:** Whether you are selling products or services, it's never been easier to build a website yourself using sites like Squarespace, WordPress, or Wix, or Shopify for product-based businesses.

- **Email Marketing Software:** Do not be one of those entrepreneurs who spend their first year of business not collecting email addresses. Your email list is one of the best investments you can make in your business. For every £1 you invest in your email list, you can expect to generate £36 in return. Why? Because those on your email list become your most loyal fans and, in turn, customers. There is lots of email marketing software available from companies, including Mailchimp, Flodesk and Convertkit. Many providers let you start for free – you only start paying for the software once your email subscriber numbers hit a certain size. Remember, people do not give their email addresses for free, so you will need to create a lead magnet. If you are running a service-based business, you could create a free download that gives subscribers some free value and offers a taste of your paid-for services. If you are running a product-based business, you can offer a discount code in exchange for an email address. The email marketing software you choose will have customisable landing page templates to advertise your

190

lead magnet, as well as email templates that will automatically deliver your lead magnet when someone signs up, so you do not manually need to send your freebie every time someone inputs their email address – phew! Your email marketing provider will also have pop-up templates you can customise to add to your website to advertise your lead magnet.

Once you have those email addresses, do not forget to nurture your subscribers by emailing them regularly – ideally weekly – so you are top of their mind when they are ready to buy the product or service you offer. You can email them links to blog posts, podcasts, or videos you have created, product round-ups, tips and advice that position you as an expert, and any offers you want to promote.

- **A Social Media Profile:** Choose the platform your ideal client is most likely to be hanging out on and spend your time there. Create a profile/page and spend time networking and commenting on other people's posts as well as creating your own posts that not only sell your products and services, and advertise your lead magnet, but also add value, position you as an expert, and create the 'know, like and trust' factor that encourages sales, referrals and repeat business.

- **A Business Bank Account:** Yes, you will need a separate bank account to keep track of income, expenditure and profit; the tax man will not be happy if you do not. And if you do not have a separate account, you also will not be able to see how well your business is doing. There are several free business bank accounts available, including ones from Tide and Starling Bank, that allow you to send invoices or accept card payments so you can get paid for all your hard work!

And that's pretty much it. I do not think when you first start out, you need to overcomplicate things by getting anything more. Do not forget to investigate if there is any support, grants or loans available for your business. Depending on your location and business type, you may be eligible for free training courses, grants or loans to buy equipment.

Be Brave, and Just Do It!

Rebecca Newenham launched her outsourcing business, Get Ahead VA, 14 years ago from home, after a career break raising her daughters and without prior business experience. During those years, Rebecca's business has gone from strength to strength. After starting her business as a solopreneur from her kitchen table, Rebecca has grown Get Ahead into an award-winning business with eight franchisees and a team of over 80 virtual experts.

Here's what Rebecca has to say about launching a business:[2]

> *'Yes, it's a scary step to start your own business. But it could be the best thing you have ever done. Once you've done your research, then just get on with it. Don't be afraid if things don't work out quite as you hoped. Keep evolving till you get it right. Over the past 14 years of running my business there have been several setbacks. But there have been so many highlights too, like winning awards, or when a client tells you what a difference your team has made. It might sometimes be a rollercoaster, but the value of working flexibly around my family makes all the hard work to run my own business worthwhile.'*

And if Rebecca, Amanda – and I – can run a business from home, around families and without investment, you can too! I genuinely believe we only regret what we do not try, so if you want to be your own boss, give it a go! You do not have to quit your job to do so. Many businesses start as side passions in the evening around an existing 9–5, with people only going full time in their business once they can replace the income they are making in their job. Start small, do not be afraid to experiment, and enjoy the ride!

Summary

Understand What Self-Employment Is – And If it's Right for You: Self-employment offers flexibility, variety, and the potential to pursue your business ideas, encompassing freelancing, contracting, franchising, or launching your own business. It allows for work around personal commitments but comes with risks, like an uncertain salary and potentially increased work hours.

Align Your Business Goals with Personal Values: Reflect on your strengths, values, and what success means to you to determine if self-employment aligns with your career goals. Consider the type of work you want to do, your ideal clients, and how you envision your work – life balance to shape your business idea.

Do Your Research: This is essential to ensuring there's a demand for your product or service. Research helps identify your ideal customer, competition, and market gaps. It's crucial to understand how to position your business uniquely and attractively.

Business Essentials: Start with minimal investment to test your business concept. Essentials include a website, email marketing software for building a customer base, a social media presence for marketing and engagement, and a separate business bank account for financial management. Seek out available support, grants, or loans that could help with your start-up phase.

Notes

1. Elizabeth Willetts (2023). Leaping into Freelancing: Amanda Henderson's Journey to Success as a Freelance HR Specialist. *Work It Like A Mum* (podcast) 29 June 2023. MP3 audio, www.buzzsprout.com/2046830/13103937.
2. Investing in Women/Rebecca Newenham (2023). https://investinginwomen .co.uk/running-your-own-business. Accessed 5 March 2024.

Chapter 20

How to Make it Work

I hate to break it to you, but life is BUSY. We all have commitments outside of work, whether it's family, pets, caring responsibilities, as well as the never-ending cooking and cleaning. And somehow, we have to fit work in to pay that mortgage or go on that nice holiday. It's not surprising that sleep, self-care, and exercise can be de-prioritised and fall down the list. I do not pretend to have things nailed by any means, but to be successful at work, you have to find some sort of balance between all your commitments – and make time for yourself so you do not get burnt out.

Since having children and launching Investing in Women, I have worked hard – really hard. And trying to work around my kids has meant lots of late nights. Sometimes so many late nights that I've made myself ill through exhaustion. I've ended up resenting work and being unable to perform at my best the next day (or for the rest of that week, if I'm being honest), so I know the risks to your career of burnout all too well. Here I'll tell you about some of the ways I find some sort of balance and manage to juggle it all in my working day.

I used to have a very unhealthy relationship with work and felt like every minute I was awake and not working was a minute wasted. Now, rather than sneaking down to my laptop before my kids wake up, I use that time to follow a 20–25-minute YouTube exercise video – something I can do first thing in my pyjamas, that's not too much effort, but that boosts my energy, clears my head, and just sets me up for the day.

Since I stopped trying to work every evening and prioritised my health, my business has flourished. But in order to carve out that time, you do need to create boundaries and set realistic expectations. We're not superhuman, we need time off to rest and recover. But we need support of some form or another to achieve that. To avoid burnout and produce your best work, I advocate putting your hand up for help, delegating where you can, and trying to remove as much from your plate as possible. It's not a sign of weakness to say you cannot do everything.

During term time, I make use of after-school clubs a couple of times a week to give me an extra hour or so during my working day. School holidays are a hodgepodge of holiday camps and grandparent help. But, being self-employed, I'm lucky I can scale back on work during the school holidays and only focus on the essentials so I can enjoy days off and time with the kids, ramping things back up again when the new term starts. I have a cleaner who cleans my house once a fortnight and someone who mows my lawn and does my weeding a couple of times a month. I know I'm fortunate to be able to afford that, but I also choose to spend my money on that rather than on other things. Having those two big jobs taken off my plate means I have more time (and headspace) to focus on my work and business, which is important to me (and the extra revenue I can generate during that time pays me more than I pay them, so it's actually a good investment). Rather than doing household chores, weekends are spent resting, recharging and spending time with my family (oh, and doing about 10 loads of washing – I have not managed to outsource everything yet), so I am fresher and have more energy when I return to work on a Monday.

Like employing people to do certain things around my home, the best investment in my business has been to employ other people who are far better at certain tasks than I am, giving me time to do other things. This has certainly saved me many late nights on Google, trying to find something out on my own that would take someone else five minutes to complete. If you are employed, ask your team or manager for help when you need it, and do not say yes to every request. If you know a certain ask will put too much strain on your time, be bold and ask your manager what work they'd like you to de-prioritise to fulfil their new request. And if you are a manager, do not feel bad; embrace delegation. It's not a sign of weakness that you cannot do everything, but rather that your time is now too valuable to spend doing certain tasks. And how will your team learn and develop if you try to hog all the work yourself?

Rachel Exton is an experienced manager at Pearson Education, in their marketing department. I asked her what were the qualities of a good manager. Here's what she said:[1]

> 'I think the thing that I have learned over the past 20 years is the importance of listening. When I was first promoted to manager, I thought I needed all the answers. It was like, "I'm a manager, so I have to know this. I have to know how to do it. I have to be the first one to speak. I have to do this." And what I realised quite quickly is that you don't need to have all the answers. And the most important thing you can do is really listen to people. Quite often, people know what the answer to their question is or the solution to a challenge, but they might not be able to articulate it correctly, or have confidence in their convictions. I really learned the power of this when I joined Pearson because I'd never worked in education previously and had grown up working in FMCG and technology companies. So, when I joined, I wasn't a subject matter expert. But what I realised is, that by listening to the team, they had all the answers. And what I could do is help them with storytelling and give them a platform to make sure the change they wanted happened.
>
> The other thing I've learned is the importance of culture champions. It was something my boss introduced me to. You can't change a culture on your own. A team is more than just

197

one person. It has to come from within. I think the loveliest defi-
nition of culture is how we do things here. But it's the way you
do it all as a collective.'

And remember, most things are not urgent. I know with emails on our phones it can be tempting to check and reply as soon as something comes in, but many people email at a time that suits them, not expecting an immediate reply.

If you are in a partnership at home, make sure your partner does their fair share. I genuinely believe women will not achieve equality in the workplace until we have equality at home. I know many couples sit down together on a Sunday to distribute the week's chores. It's not the most romantic thing to do, but it does save a lot of arguments.

I also advocate that if you can, pay for a cleaner. For many people, if they worked out their hourly wage, it would make financial sense to pay a cleaner for a couple of hours a week. Honestly, it transforms your weekends and time off if you do not have that pressure and niggling voice in the back of your head saying 'you need to clean the house'. Even if you can just afford a cleaner once a fortnight (which I do), it takes the pressure off me from thinking that I need to spend my Saturday cleaning the bathroom – and I can use that time to rest and recharge after a busy week at work.

Many people also advocate for batch cooking, ordering food online rather than going to the shops, and not stressing if your house does not look like a show home the entire time!

If you have children, the best way to thrive both at work and at home is to 'build a village' that can support you, whether that's helping with pick-ups (perhaps a neighbour you can take turns with), emergency childcare if your child is sick, fetching you food if you get sick, or even just a friendly face for moral support when you are dealing with the umpteenth tantrum of the day.

For many people, the most important person in their village is their partner, but the village could also comprise grandparents, neighbours, or other parents at the school gate. The village could also be paid, such as the cleaner, the food delivery guy, a childminder, or a nanny. You cannot do it all – nor should you. So, think about how you can build a village that will give you space for you – and your career.

Case Study – Rosie Reynolds, Chief Commercial Officer of Aspect Capital

Rosie Reynolds is a mum of four and the COO of Aspect Capital, a London-based systematic investment manager. When her youngest child was 12 months old, she was offered a big promotion that was a stepping stone to a board role:[2]

> 'I've always had a conflict between wanting to be the best mother I can to my children and at the same time, doing the very best for Aspect. I've always been of the view that family comes first, so struggle with that dichotomy. How can I be a good parent and do my best at work? When my youngest was born, family life was incredibly busy as my husband is a partner in a law firm and works long hours. But this opportunity came up, and Anthony, our CEO, rang me and asked if I would consider taking on the role, which was essentially the chance I'd been waiting for my entire career: if I was to have any role in the organisation, it was that one. However, with four children under eight years old and a somewhat chaotic home life, I honestly felt I wasn't in a position to deliver what Aspect needed, but felt hugely conflicted and didn't want to let the opportunity pass. I was open about the situation and Anthony said, "Take a few more months maternity leave, and then let's discuss how we might be able to make this work for all of us. Reflect on what you require to feel supported

How to Make it Work

and maintain a good work/life balance, and we'll make it work." So, over time, we agreed how the role could work, and then, armed with a flexible working arrangement, I felt ready to return. Aspect also invested in some executive coaching sessions for me, which were invaluable.

Before I met my coach, Charlotte, I very much viewed the world in absolutes, which to my mind meant that to be a good mother, I needed to be with my children 24/7, and if I wasn't doing that, the children would be suffering. My mum didn't work; she was always at home, and that was my role model. Charlotte encouraged me to see things in a less black-and-white manner and suggested I consider a "quality vs quantity" approach to family life. Organising my home life more efficiently and also prioritising some time for me, whether that was just a couple of hours a week to gather my thoughts or go to the gym, was essential.

Charlotte showed me the importance of focusing on myself first so that I could contribute what I needed at home and work. I consider myself a very organised person. But she said, "No, I think you can be more disciplined. Every Sunday night, sit down. Map out your diary for the next month with your husband so you don't have any moments where you are in conflict over who does what." We've taken that to the extreme – our diaries are now mapped out 6–12 months ahead, but home life runs far more smoothly!

Charlotte suggested we got a cleaner to remove some pressure at home. We were also fortunate to have a nanny. With two big jobs and four children, this was transformational. With so many children, for us it was financially easier than paying for after-school care and places at nursery and had the added benefit of arriving home to a tidy house and children ready for bed.

My advice to other parents worried about juggling work and career would be to go for it. The dynamics at home shift as children get older and the juggle does get easier. If you can establish a good set-up at home and work and get that running smoothly, there's no reason why you can't push for promotion. I used to think of all the reasons why it "wouldn't work" rather than "how it might work". So, if you've decided that you want to shoot for the stars and now's the moment, just go for it. Explore flexible working arrangements with your employer. Even small adjustments to your working day can make a huge difference to your work/life balance, and they don't need to be forever – whatever it takes to get you through to the next phase of parenthood. Make sure you've got the right support network in place at home, do whatever you can to make life more efficient (there is always something!), and secure additional help – whether it's through your partner, a nursery, nanny, or cleaner. And stock up on the ready meals!'

Some of the best career advice I've seen being given to young women who want to combine parenthood with a career is to find the right partner – one who will support you and pull their weight at home. But not everyone is lucky enough to have a supportive partner – or even a partner at all. In fact, according to the Office of National Statistics, there are 2.9 million lone-parent families in 2022: 2.5 million (84%) headed by a lone mother and 457,000 (16%) by a lone father.[3] If you are a single parent, hats off to you – I do not know how you do it. You're amazing. It's hard not to have someone around to help out at bath or bedtime, share the school run, or even take the kids to the park so you can put your feet up for an hour or so. Give yourself a big pat on the back for everything you are doing.

Rosemarie Fox, an HR business partner at Saint-Gobain, is a single mum to her son, Noah. I asked her how she made time for herself as a single parent, and here's what she said:[4]

'As you know, with kids, you're just continuously washing clothes. So you need to carve out some time for yourself when you get your child down for bed, even if it's just 30 minutes. You sometimes have to force yourself to do it because if you don't, you're going to be up getting the uniform and the lunch ready for tomorrow, but you just actually have to take a debrief.

I've got better at it over the years. It does take time because you're always trying to be one step ahead. But I always find something happens if you try to be one step ahead. So you're better off actually taking that 30 minutes watching the silliest programme. I watch some silly programmes because they don't require me to think too much. Just a comedy that's 30 minutes long. You laugh, and you know, when it's over, you can get back up and feel re-energised. It could be a book for someone, but you have to take that time for yourself.

My mam told me one thing when I'd just had Noah. She said, "I don't want to be looking at you in this house every weekend. Get yourself a good childminder and get yourself back into work. Find two or three babysitters that you're happy to use and get out at the weekends because if you don't do that, parenthood will consume you."

And she was saying that as a woman who had three children. And I actually remember that as a child, we used to have babysitters, and on a Saturday, every so often, my mam and dad would go out and enjoy themselves. And I think that was their reboot. So many people feel guilty going out and leaving their children, but it's the best thing ever because your child is actually seeing you go out, enjoy yourself and come back, re-energised and putting your energy back into them on a Sunday.'

It's not just a case of trying to fit everything in – it's also about enjoying life. It's about forgetting FOMO, enjoying all of life's moments and being present – whatever you are doing. Things can wait. Unless you are a doctor in A&E, nothing is an emergency, and no one expects a response right at this minute.

Nicola Lee is a sales manager with Jewson. She had just been promoted to a much bigger job when her twins were toddlers, and her mum gave her this advice about being present:[5]

> 'I remember one day when my twins were about two, and I came home from work, and my mum said to me, "I understand that you have got a big job. You've got a much better job than I had at your age with children. But I want you to know that when you're in the house, you have to be present in front of your kids. You can't just be on the phone. You can't be trying to sort customer problems because your children, when they know that mummy is in the room, just want their mum. And they want their dad when their dad's in the room. As you come down the path, turn your phone off and be present." And I think that was really great advice to have because otherwise, you can be really important and busy somewhere else, rather than the place you're really needed at that precise moment.'

Nicola Lee's reflections about the importance of being present and mindful of how you spend your time away from work echo a much broader theme of balance and authenticity – something many people aspire to but also find challenging. Sarah McMath is the CEO of MOSL. I asked her what her advice would be to others wanting to be themselves and advocate for their needs so they could thrive at work. Here's what she said:[6]

> 'I would advise people to be honest and open about what they need to do to be their best, authentic self every day and to deliver – and to have those conversations. If I have one regret it's that I wasn't. I remember, early on in my career, going home early for a sports day or something to do with school, and leaving

my jacket on my chair, and hoping, "Oh, they'll think I'm at a meeting or something."

So, I would ask people to be honest. And if that honesty leads you to a position of being uncomfortable, then ideally, the organisation changes.

But find an organisation that wants you. I managed to make it work in difficult circumstances. But there are lots of great companies out there who embrace flexible working. I don't think anyone should have to pretend to try and survive in a job. You're at work for a long time. You're a grown-up for a very long time. I would urge people to find an organisation that respects you.'

The good news is that companies are becoming increasingly flexible and conscious of employee needs and their health and well-being. And like Sarah, I believe that if your employer does not understand its obligations to you as a person – perhaps they are not the employer for you after all.

Navigating the demands of a bustling life – balancing career, home, and personal growth – can seem like a never-ending challenge. In this chapter, we have delved into practical strategies and personal insights to help you manage this juggle more effectively. Whether it's embracing the support of a 'village', setting realistic boundaries at work, or ensuring you carve out time for yourself, the goal is clear: to thrive in ALL areas of your life without burnout. Remember, the journey towards achieving a work–life balance is a continuous one, peppered with learning, adjustments, and flexibility (in all areas of life). It's also about lowering your expectations and not trying to do it all! Try to integrate some of these practices into your daily routine, and watch as they gradually transform your approach to managing both your personal and professional commitments. By cultivating an environment of support and understanding, both at home and in the workplace, you'll pave the way for not only surviving – but thriving in all areas of your life!

Summary

Acknowledge Life Is Busy: Life is inherently busy, filled with commitments that range from family responsibilities to self-care and professional obligations. Recognising this allows us to approach our daily routines with a mindset that seeks balance rather than perfection.

Set Boundaries and Delegate: To prevent burnout and maintain productivity, it's crucial to set clear boundaries between work and personal life, delegate tasks effectively, and ask for help when needed. This not only improves your personal well-being but also increases work efficiency.

Build a Supportive Village: Creating a 'village' of support, including partners, family, childcare providers, and even a cleaner, can significantly reduce the strain of daily tasks. This support network is essential for balancing the various demands of work and home life – and preventing burnout and stress.

Be Present and Mindful: Being present and putting the phone away helps ensure that time spent with family is quality time, enriching relationships and reducing stress.

Find Flexible and Supportive Work Environments: It's important to work for an organisation that respects and supports your need for flexibility. An understanding workplace can significantly contribute to your ability to manage work and personal life effectively – and thrive in your career!

Notes

1. Elizabeth Willetts (2024). Can You Really Have It All? Debunking Career Myths with Rachel Exton. *Work It Like A Mum* (podcast) 2 May 2024. mp3 audio, 46:44, www.buzzsprout.com/2046830/14992698-can-you-

really-have-it-all-debunking-career-myths-with-rachel-exton. Accessed 5 August 2024.

2. Elizabeth Willetts (2024). 'I felt like an imposter for a long time in my career – now I'm the COO of a leading Asset Management firm'. *Work It Like A Mum* (podcast) 1 December 2024. MP3 audio, 47:09, www.buzzsprout .com/2046830/11756406.

3. Office of National Statistics (2022). Families and households in the UK. www .ons.gov.uk/peoplepopulationandcommunity/birthsdeathsandmarriages/ families/bulletins/familiesandhouseholds/2022. Accessed 5 August 2024.

4. Elizabeth Willetts (2024). Finding Your Village: How to Build a Support Network – AND a Thriving Career as a Single Parent With Rosemarie Fox. *Work It Like A Mum* (podcast) 11 April 2024. MP3 audio, 34:09, www.buzzsprout .com/2046830/14863849.

5. Elizabeth Willetts (2024). Want to Thrive in Your Career After Kids? Here's How One Woman Crushed It (And Even a Cancer Diagnosis Hasn't Stopped Her. *Work It Like A Mum* (podcast) 21 March 2024. MP3 audio, 41:33, www .buzzsprout.com/2046830/14732476-want-to-thrive-in-your-career-after- kids-here-s-how-one-woman-crushed-it-and-even-a-cancer-diagnosis-hasn- t-stopped-her. Accessed 5 August 2024.

6. Elizabeth Willetts (2022). How to Get What You Really Want in Your Career – Top Tips from a CEO Who's Made It to the Top of Her Male- Dominated Industry – Whilst Working Part-Time. *Work It Like A Mum* (podcast) 24 November 2022. MP3 audio, 48.07, www.buzzsprout .com/2046830/11663396. Accessed 5 August 2024.

Final Thoughts

Embracing the Journey

As we come to the close of this journey together, it's important to reflect on the key themes that have woven through the chapters of this book. Whether you're stepping into the workforce for the first time, navigating mid-career changes, or looking to pivot entirely, the landscape of modern work is both challenging and ripe with opportunity.

Empowerment Through Information: Each chapter of this book has been designed to equip you with the knowledge, strategies, and insights needed to navigate today's complex job market. From crafting standout CVs and acing interviews to negotiating pay rises and embracing flexibility, the goal has been to empower you to take charge of your career and destiny.

Flexibility and Forward Thinking: We've explored the importance of flexibility in the workplace. How it's not just a perk but a necessity for so many in the modern work environment. The shift towards more dynamic work arrangements offers a chance to redesign not just when and where we work, but how we can achieve our best results without sacrificing our well-being. And hopefully the chapter on making a flexible working request will enable you to get the working pattern that works best for you and your circumstances – and enable you to thrive!

Building Resilience and Adaptability: The stories I've shared throughout the book have highlighted the importance of being resilient and adaptable as crucial skills when navigating your career. Whether it's overcoming setbacks, managing personal challenges while maintaining professional growth, or simply learning to thrive in diverse environments, resilience stands out as a key driver of long-term success.

The Power of Networking: We've discussed the undeniable power of building and nurturing a professional network. Networking is not just about expanding your professional contacts but about building genuine relationships that can offer support, provide mentorship, and open doors to opportunities that might not be accessible otherwise.

Commitment to Continuous Learning: In a world that is constantly changing, the commitment to lifelong learning is more important than ever. This book has hopefully inspired you to continue growing your skills, whether through formal education, self-directed learning, or professional experiences.

Advocacy for Equality: Lastly, I've tried to strongly advocate for equality in the workplace throughout this book. Achieving professional heights is only meaningful when we pave the way for others to succeed. Please don't ever pull the ladder up behind you. We all have a responsibility to push for policies that ensure fair treatment, respect, and equal opportunities for all, regardless of gender, ethnicity, background, or life circumstances.

As you turn the final page, remember that your career is a marathon, not a sprint. It's a personal journey that's as unique as you are – and that's what makes it exciting. It's never too late to try something new. Keep setting goals, pushing boundaries, and staying true to your values. Here's to your success – on your terms!

Thank you for allowing me to be a part of your career journey. I hope the chapters you've explored inspire you to build the professional life you deserve – one that's filled with achievements, fulfilment, and, most of all, joy.

CV Template

First Name, Surname

Postal Address, Email Address, Phone Number, LinkedIn Profile
(if applicable)

Quick Biography – Who are you, what have you done,
what is your key experience? (Keep this to 2–3 lines)

Career

Job Title   **Dates employed from–until**

Employer   *(Keep month format consistent*
and write present if still there)

- List all your day-to-day responsibilities using bullet points to make it easier to read.
- Avoid generalisations.
- Do you manage anyone; if so, how many? Who do you report to (their job title not their actual name)?
- Refer back to the job advert to make sure you include all the keywords asked for (remember, your CV has to potentially get past an automated computer sift before an actual person reviews it!).

Key Achievements

Include some key achievements for every single job.

- How did you make a positive impact in your job that was unique to you?
- Use the STAR technique when writing about these achievements – be **S**pecific, about the **T**ask, what you **A**chieved, and the **R**esult. (Refer to Chapter 7 'Writing a CV' for more advice on this.)

Now repeat the above for all recent jobs in reverse chronological order. For jobs that are no longer relevant, or took place a long time ago, include one bullet point covering your main duty. If you were employed for a period doing various temporary jobs that are not relevant to this application, write the following header:

Various temporary jobs   **Dates employed from–until**

Education

Include any professional qualifications (ACA, CIMA, CIPD, etc.) you may have.

Qualfication (BSc, A Levels, BTEC, etc.) Dates studied from–until
Name of institution

Keep repeating the above until you reach A Levels (or equivalent)

IT Skills

Word, Excel (how advanced?), PowerPoint, Outlook, any other specialist systems knowledge

Languages

If you speak any languages in addition to English, write them here including proficiency level

Full Driving Licence (if applicable and required for the job you are applying for)

* * *

Here's the link to download your free CV template – https://investinginwomen .co.uk/our-freebies/free-cv-template/.

Cover Letter Template

Dear (Hiring Manager name), (if known)

Dear Sir or Madam, (if name unavailable)

I am writing to express my keen interest in the (Job Title) position advertised on (Website where you saw the job posting). With (Number) years of experience in (Your relevant field), I am confident I possess the skills and qualifications you are seeking for the position.

Here are some highlights of my achievements that demonstrate my capabilities and the value I can bring to your organisation:

- **Achievement 1 using the STAR method:** Briefly describe the situation, task, action taken, and the positive result, showcasing a skill relevant to the job.
- **Achievement 2 using the STAR method:** Briefly describe the situation, task, action taken, and the positive result, showcasing a second skill relevant to the job.
- **Achievement 3 using STAR method (Optional):** Briefly describe the situation, task, action taken, and the positive result, showcasing a third skill relevant to the job.

(Company Name) is a highly respected company in the (Industry) industry, and I have been particularly impressed by (something specific about the company that caught your attention, e.g. a recent project, CSR initiatives, social media campaigns, their company culture).

My skills in (List 3–4 relevant skills from the job description) align perfectly with the requirements outlined in the job advertisement, and I am confident I will be able to quickly add value to your organisation.

In addition to the above, I am a highly motivated and results-oriented individual with a strong work ethic and a passion for (your area of expertise). I am confident that I can make a significant contribution to (Company Name)'s continued success.

Thank you for your time and consideration. I am available for an interview at your earliest convenience and can be reached at (Phone number) or (Email address).

Yours sincerely, (if you used the person's name in the greeting)

Yours faithfully, (if you used Dear Sir or Madam in the greeting)

Your name

One Month's Worth of LinkedIn Post Prompts

Motivational Monday

Starting the week with a positive mindset and a brisk morning walk/ favourite coffee/gym class or something about what you did over the weekend. Don't forget to ask your network what they got up to, to spark conversation (and engagement) in the comments.

Or... my favourite quote to kick off the week is (Inspirational Quote). It reminds me of (Personal Insight). What's your go-to quote for motivation?

Industry News Reaction

Just stumbled upon this piece about (Recent Industry Development) and wow, it's a game-changer! It reminds me of that time I (Personal Career Experience). What are your thoughts on this?

Career Milestone

Can you believe it? It's been (Number) years in (Industry/Profession)! From my early days of (Personal Anecdote) to now, the journey's been nothing short of amazing. Biggest lesson so far? (Key Lesson.) What's a career highlight you're most proud of?

Networking Call to Action

I'm on a mission to meet new faces in (Industry/Sector) (and maybe share a coffee or two). If you're up for a chat and some idea-swapping, let's connect!

Skill Development

Diving into (New Skill or Course) and mixing it up with my love for (Personal Hobby/Interest). I can't wait to see how this levels up my

(Professional Skill/Service). Fellow (Professionals/Hobbyists) – what am I letting myself into? Any wisdom to share?

Behind-the-Scenes

Ever wondered what a day in the life of a (Your Profession) looks like? Well, it starts with (Personal Morning Routine) and then... (write about your day). Let's compare notes! How do your working days shape up? Anything I'm missing?

Industry Tip Tuesday

Here's a little Tuesday wisdom from my own 'oops' moments: (Share a Quick Tip related to your field plus face plant emoji). Learned this one the hard way (and how what you learnt from it shaped your career)! What's been your biggest oops moment – and what did you learn from it?

Work–Life Balance

Juggling (Personal Interest/Hobby/Family) with a busy (Your Profession) career – not always easy, but worth it. How do you keep the balance? I'm all ears for new strategies that help manage the juggle!

Client Testimonial/Feedback

Just got some feedback that made my day: (Insert Testimonial). It's moments like these that remind me why I love what I do. Ever had feedback that just made you smile all day?

Book Recommendation

Finished (Book Name) by (Author) and it's amazing – it completely changed my way of thinking! Perfect for anyone in (Field/Industry) or anyone who loves (Personal Interest). Here's why it's a must-read...

Success Story

Super excited to share a recent win: (Describe a Successful Project/Achievement). This one was close to my heart because it resonated with my belief in (Personal Values). Here's the scoop...

Industry Event Reflection

I had a blast at (Event/Conference) last week. The highlight? Definitely (Session Topic) with (tag the speaker). Took me back to (Personal Experience/Anecdote). Any of you there? Would love to hear your takeaways.

Throwback Thursday

Throwback to this amazing moment: (Past Experience/Project). It was a real game-changer for me, both professionally and personally because... What's one of your favourite work-related memories?

Poll Post

Quick poll: What's the biggest head-scratcher in (Your Industry/Field) right now? (List Options). Your insights are gold – they might even help me with my upcoming (Personal Project/Initiative).

Friday Reflection

Wrapping up the week with (Personal Activity) this weekend. This week's big lesson? (Professional Learning). How do you wind down and reflect?

Collaboration Call-out

On the lookout for some brilliant minds to collaborate with in (Area of Interest). If you're into (Related Project/Field) and/or (Personal Interest/Hobby), let's connect and make some magic happen!

Personal Story

Storytime! Here's a little something about (Personal Topic) that's had a big impact on my work life. It's all about (Specific Way it Influenced Work). Ever had a similar experience?

Question Post

Just wondering: (Ask a Thought-Provoking Question related to your field). Eager to hear your thoughts – your insights could inspire my next (Personal Project/Interest). Let's get the conversation rolling!

Gratitude Post

Today, I'm feeling thankful for (Aspect of Work/Professional Relationship/Award). It's these moments that make everything worth it. What's something in your professional life that you're grateful for?

Monday Goals

New week, new goals! On my list: (List Professional Goals) and on a personal note, aiming to (Personal Goal). Inspire me! What are you setting your sights on this week?

Flexible Working Request Template

Subject: Request for Flexible Working Arrangements

Dear (Manager's Name),

I am writing to formally request a change in my current working arrangements. In accordance with the Flexible Working (Amendment) Regulations 2023, I would like to propose the following adjustments to my working pattern, effective from (Proposed Start Date).

Current Working Pattern:

Detail your current working hours, days, and any specific patterns relevant to your current role.

Proposed Working Pattern:

Detail the specific changes you are requesting. This might include part-time hours, specific days working from home, staggered hours, etc. Be as specific as possible.

Reason for Request:

And although you're no longer required to, explaining your reasons for requesting these changes gives more context to your employer and will encourage them to say yes. Focus on how these changes will maintain or improve your work performance and benefit the team and company.

Potential Impact on the Business and Proposed Solutions:

Discuss any potential impact your proposed changes might have on your role and the broader team. Offer practical solutions to mitigate these impacts. For example, if you propose to work from home, explain how you will maintain communication and productivity.

Benefits to the Employer:
Highlight the potential benefits to the employer, such as increased productivity, improved employee well-being, or alignment with company values of diversity and flexibility.

Trial Period:
I am open to the idea of a trial period to assess the effectiveness of the proposed working pattern. I suggest a trial period of (suggest a period, e.g. 3–6 months), after which we could review the arrangement, my performance and make any necessary adjustments.

I am committed to ensuring a seamless transition should my request be approved and am open to discussing any concerns or suggestions you may have regarding this proposal.
Thank you for considering my request. I am hopeful for a positive response and am available for a meeting to discuss this further at your earliest convenience.

Yours sincerely,
Your Name

* * *

You can find a free flexible working request template at: https://investinginwomen.co.uk/our-freebies/free-flexible-working-request-template.

About the Author

Elizabeth Willetts is the Founder of Investing in Women – a female-empowering and award-winning job board and community helping family-friendly AND forward-thinking employers hire professionals looking for fulfilling, flexible, and part-time work. She is an experienced recruiter with over 18 years of experience – both in-house at one of the Big 4 and from one of the UK's largest recruitment agencies. Elizabeth is also a mum to two daughters – Emily and Annabelle (and a Labradoodle called Dougal). She is a passionate believer in the power of part-time and flexible work to retain women in the workplace and close the gender pay gap.